The Twelve Initiations With Mary Magdalene

The Twelve Initiations
with
Mary Magdalene

A Journey of Self-Discovery and Empowerment

LUCI WILLIAMS

The Twelve Initiations with Mary Magdalene,
A Journey of Self-Discovery and Empowerment
Published by Peace Flower Publishing
Alachua, Florida, U.S.A.

Copyright ©2023, LUCI WILLIAMS. All rights reserved.

No part of this book may be reproduced in any form or by any mechanical means, including information storage and retrieval systems without permission in writing from the publisher/author, except by a reviewer who may quote passages in a review. All images, logos, quotes, and trademarks included in this book are subject to use according to trademark and copyright laws of the United States of America.

WILLIAMS, LUCI, Author
THE TWELVE INITIATIONS WITH MARY MAGDALENE
LUCI WILLIAMS

Library of Congress Control Number: 2023908581

ISBN: 979-8-9883303-0-1 (paperback)
ISBN: 979-8-9883303-2-5 (paperback)
ISBN: 979-8-9883303-1-8 (digital)

BODY, MIND & SPIRIT / Healing / Prayer & Spiritual
RELIGION / Biblical Meditations / General
SELF-HELP / Spiritual

Copy Editor: Robin Fuller
Product Manager: Olga Anisimova
Interior Book Designer: Daphney Milian
Publishing Consultant: Susie Schaefer (finishthebookpublishing.com)
Cover Image Attributed to Nicholas Roerich, 1924, Mother of the World, Матерь Мира (original title)
The art is currently held in Roerich Museum, Moscow, Russia.

QUANTITY PURCHASES: Schools, companies, professional groups, clubs, and other organizations may qualify for special terms when ordering quantities of this title. For information, email: peaceflowerpublishing@protonmail.com.

All rights reserved by LUCI WILLIAMS and PEACE FLOWER PUBLISHING.
This book is printed in the United States of America.

Dedicated to...

You. The holy, divine presence of all that You Are. Thank you for taking this dive, this wild choice to become human and to experience physical life on Earth. Thank you for your radiant, unique light that only you offer to this incredible reality. Thank you for your pure and beautiful heart, your sacred intentions, and your holy efforts in life. Thank you for your interest in knowing yourself more deeply. This book is dedicated to you and all that You Are.

CONTENTS

INTRODUCTION	9
INITIATION ONE	19
INITIATION TWO	33
INITIATION THREE	45
INITIATION FOUR	57
INITIATION FIVE	69
INITIATION SIX	81
INITIATION SEVEN	99
INITIATION EIGHT	111
INITIATION NINE	125
INITIATION TEN	139
INITIATION ELEVEN	149
INITIATION TWELVE	165

A MESSAGE FROM THE AUTHOR

This book is a feeling experience, to know more of yourself, to expand into aspects that may seem fantastical or unreal, solely for the imprinting this memory will make on the body, the remembering of who you truly are - that you're more than what you've been told, more than what you see with your eyes, more than this body, more than this reality...

Please enjoy this book.

It came out of the most blissful interaction with the energy I know as ascended master Mary Magdalene. It is my sincere desire that you will feel the joy, the awe, and the unconditional love with which this book was created.

I have been asking the question for several years now, who am I? This question would often lead me to deep meditations where I would meet guides from the nonphysical realms who would offer gifts and wisdom, open my heart, and walk me through events and experiences that would help me gain clarity and perspective.

These experiences were powerful and moving, yet how I felt in these moments was very different from how I felt in my daily life. It was like I was living two lives. I wanted to unify all that I was, and show up in every scenario as the fullest light of my divine presence.

I asked again, with all my passion: who am I?

Mary Magdalene came through. Her voice was so easy to hear, so loving. I began meditating with her regularly, calling on her specifically to help me understand more of who I truly am, and to help me move through moments of confusion or challenges in my life. Her gentle unwavering acceptance of all that I am would move me to tears. She would repeatedly ask me to think of her as my sister, my equal, not a goddess or anyone "higher" than myself. She would often remind me that I am more than I know. With her help I began to see even more of who I truly am, to trust this, and integrate this into my everyday life.

I was on a phone call with close friends in September of 2021, when out of nowhere I heard the instruction, "you are going to write a book with Mary Magdalene". I could feel my whole body zinging wildly in excitement at the thought of it, paired with surprise at such an unusual idea—I wasn't an author. Several weeks later I was in Maryland on a jog in the middle of a beautiful park when I heard her voice clearly in my ears:

We will write the Twelve Initiations together.

I loved this idea! Again I was overcome with elation and delight, and simultaneously wondering, how would this happen?

When I sat down for the first writing session, I didn't know what to expect. I felt only awe and gratitude, knowing it was my greatest joy to spend time with Mary Magdalene. What unfolded during the next eight weeks (while staying in Mary-Land) was an incredible experience of discovery and expansion, as she personally guided me through the Twelve Initiations.

For each initiation, we would start standing in the center of a circle with twelve points around it. She would walk with me to the doorway and let me enter on my own, always assuring me that she was with me, even if I couldn't see her. The beautiful places and otherworldly beings surprised and delighted me. Each initiation was its own unique adventure. Thus, I lived the experiences you are about to embark upon, hearing, seeing, touching, and smelling everything as if I were physically present.

I invite you to do the same.

You may find it fun or helpful to create a ritual before beginning, something you can do each time that signals to your body that you're entering the expansion space. It can be as simple as taking three deep breaths, putting your hands in prayer position, or lighting a candle. For me, it was putting on headphones. Whether or not I listened to any music, putting on headphones became a signal to my body that I was entering the "other" space, and it continues to work now anytime I want to go into a meditative state. Whatever you choose, let it be the same thing each time and this mudra will become empowered to easily cue your body to relax into the space of expansion.

I invite you to center in your heart, honor the beauty and wonderfulness that you are, and feel the Creator's deep gratitude and love for you.

This is a journey of self-discovery and empowerment.

Huge blessings on your initiations.

Luci

AN INTRODUCTION FROM MARY MAGDALENE

Welcome to the Twelve Initiations. I am Mary Magdalene. In my time on Earth, initiations were experiential events to guide the initiates deeper into the truth of who they were. Each initiation was intended to assist the growth of the individual, whether this meant facing a fear, expanding into deeper levels of feeling, or receiving wisdom to expand their consciousness and widen their perspective. We called it the "Golden Ladder," the ascension pathway that takes a soul to higher and higher realms of existence, ultimately to return with Source in celebration of beingness. Knowing oneself more greatly helped to expand the soul's growth while in the physical form of the human body.

Initiations helped us to remember who we were, to break through the constructs of human life—whether fears, imposed limitations, or collective beliefs—and to get closer to the fullness of our multidimensional beingness. All would be in perfect resonance for each individual's soul growth point, for the nature of initiations is to work with the current level of consciousness of each initiate.

There is much that can be done in nonphysical reality, the space that feels like it is in the mind or imagination. From many perspectives, there is no difference between what is occurring in nonphysical reality and what is occurring in your physical reality. You are invited to trust that what occurs within the space of nonphysical reality is as powerful as you may hope, and likely more so than you could imagine. Feel this trust now wash over you like a soft breeze, your muscles releasing into even more trust.

The following Twelve Initiations represent a palette of colors, expressions, explorations, and directions that shape and expand the initiate's understanding of Self. When we know who we are and what we are capable of, we allow ourselves the delight of expanding fully into the truth of who we are, thereby contributing our greatest light to Earth, as seen by higher vibrational frequencies.

Everything is vibration. Our Essene culture knew that by creating a teaching system which allowed each individual to find their own path to their highest vibration, this would have the greatest effect on the individual, our community, and even the planetary vibration. Everything is connected, as you will learn if you are yet unaware of this truth, and our Earthly vibration as self, community, and planet is most important for the greater awakening and highest potential of the individual, as well as to everything in existence on its path of climbing the Golden Ladder.

Allow yourself the curiosity of wondering what each initiation may hold for you. Allow yourself the playful space of believing it is real. Allow yourself to observe what you may find uncomfortable, and allow the remembering, that you're exploring, for fun, and for your greatest liberation and expansion.

In each of these initiations, I will walk with you to the doorway, and then leave you to have the experience on your own. Know that I am always with you, always supporting you—even when you can't see me. I am the voice guiding you through. If you find yourself on a journey all your own, outside the words being spoken, trust this. Delight in your unique flow here, knowing your own Source and guiding lights are working with you in the most perfect way.

Allow yourself the knowing that all initiations are safe, and that in all moments, even uncomfortable ones, you are being watched and loved and supported by leagues of angels, a host of personal guides, and all of us here who are helping from the vibration of unconditional love. Relax into this. Trust this. And delight in this level of support that is always, always present for you.

This is a way to engage with more of who you are. This is a way to push your edges a little, to break through your thresholds. Some initiations may seem fantastical. Just allow. Allow as if it is the more real reality. And if this feels silly or difficult, allow that! Know that you cannot do them "wrong," for there is no such thing—only learning. If you perceive them as silly, you have total freedom to close the book and find a more fun way to spend your time. And you have our blessing to do so!

There are numerous ways to enjoy this book, and each initiation may have more to offer upon the second, third, fifth, or tenth readings. Let your heart guide you to what delights you most in this process. It is the time of the Great Shedding of old fears, stories, constructs, and limits as we move into the Age of Connection and Light, and this can be a light and even delightful experience.

There is no way to do this wrong, we emphasize, for the tendency for human beings to doubt themselves, second-guess, or even experience anger towards the self for not doing something "right" is very pervasive. Know that when these feelings arise, there is a great gift lying beneath them. As you embrace them, knowing they are a sign that there is more life, more love for you beneath them, you also heal humanity of this rampant disease of self-doubt. Bless you for this great work!

We are honored that you will take these initiations with us. As you will see, there are many who came together to make this possible. Know that it is each character's greatest joy to be of service in this way to you.

You are the star of this story. You are the one we are all honoring, witnessing, and serving. And we do this because we know how great you are. We know Who You Are.

Perhaps the best way to approach each initiation is to start with a knowing that (1) this is the best thing you can be doing for yourself, and (2) a whole host of us are lovingly participating to create each experience for you. This knowing will allow for a foundational feeling of safety, which is most important. All that occurs within these initiations is of the highest light vibration of pure unconditional love. This means that whatever happens is the best for all involved. Even when moments seem uncomfortable, return to (1) the trust that this is the best thing you can do for yourself, and (2) the trust that a whole host of us are lovingly participating with you.

Another perspective is to approach the initiations with a feeling of innocence and curiosity, like a child of five or six would. Curiously explore each initiation with wonder and imagination. This allows for natural receptivity, and a deeper experiencing of each part of yourself. Ultimately, the initiations are a palette of colorful experiences to lead you to knowing more of who you truly are. As you discover your own multifaceted, multicolored nature, you feel more you-ness—and this is it! This is the vibration that blesses the planet and all within it: when you are You. I and all the loving guides participating here deeply desire for you to know the bliss of who you truly are, and these are the first Twelve Initiations to guide you in this direction.

Awareness of Being is the great gift bestowed on us by our Creator creating creation. There is great bliss in this awareness, and in realizing that simply being is our gift to creation, to life, and to Earth, knowing the gift of life is also bliss. So, here we are: immersed in bliss before we have even begun. But there is more... There is always more upon the Golden Ladder of consciousness expanding.

I leave you now with a full heart and delighted anticipation of what is to come, for both of us. I will guide you through each initiation. I will be the soft voice in your ear, leading you through the experiences. You will never be without me. You will always be safe. You will always be loved. You are always loved.

You are love.

I love you.

Mary Magdalene

Initiation One

The Twelve Initiations are circular, the sphere of totality of One's Self, which is God-self, for the One is the All.

Fractal patterns—this is the One, as all, fractalized down through space and time.

The God-self is the Oneself: One's Self.

There is a sphere here encircling the God-self, which we will refer to as You.

You are the God-self in this image.

Be the center of it.

See yourself here, the One Self that is you.

Around this sphere are twelve points. To simplify, let's imagine a two-dimensional circle, with the points like those on a clock.

You are standing in the center of this circle, and the light beam from your heart focus, your attention, shines like the spoke of a bicycle wheel, connecting you directly to point one on the circle.

You are aimed here, connected here, focused here.

Now follow the pathway of light shone by your heart as we walk to this point ONE on the circle.

As you get closer, you begin to perceive a temple ahead of you, rising from the flat clock landscape. It is a grand structure made of dark stone, towering before you. It may remind you of a cathedral, with an arched gray door of wood and metal in the center. You walk up several stone steps leading to this door, and reverently push it open.

Inside, it is dimly lit and mysterious, as if filled with fog or candle smoke, yet you feel safe. As your eyes adjust, you take another step forward. The space feels empty, all your own. It feels holy. And with the dim lighting, it is a little activating to your nervous system, and you feel excited, as in the sweetness of anticipation.

You pause and take three deep breaths here:

        In — out

        In — out

        In — out

You feel your body relaxing as your eyes adjust to the dimness. You are safe here. You feel comfortable closing the door behind you, and you do this now.

INITIATION ONE

Your eyes have now adjusted more completely, and you begin to notice the beauty all around you. Many great sculptors and artists have contributed to this place of holiness that you find yourself in now. You notice your sensitivity to these great works of art and feel grateful to be in their presence.

You take a few steps forward, and for the first time, you notice the echo of your own footfalls on the floor as you walk. It feels majestic, that your steps can create a sound wave that touches all these works of art, the towering walls, even the highest point of the ceiling. You feel connected to this place now, vibrationally, as if it is actively touching your outer energy fields. This feels empowering. You feel calm and easy here.

As you are drawn to walk to the center of this place, you allow your head to turn in all directions, taking in the myriad details of stonework, art, woodwork, sculpture, and tapestry. You let the visions of these pieces wash over you like soothing waves, restoring something within you. You feel small in this vast, echoing space, and at the same time big, for your connection to this place is quickly expanding.

You find yourself standing in the center of a circle of stones laid in a beautiful design on the floor. Looking up to the very tip-top of the spire above you, you notice a round skylight at the peak of this highest point of the ceiling. This circular window is divided into four segments by a simple vertical and horizontal line crossing through the middle. The crown of your head notices this natural light and welcomes it into your body.

You are here.

Your body knows. Your body is grateful. Your body is delighted! But your mind has no idea. Revel in this unusual moment: your body feeling so grateful, even elated to be here, and your mind wondering all the while, What is this, why, where, who…? and all the other things it wants to know. What a peculiar state to observe!

Your body is now drawn towards the far end of the temple. You can see an altar there amidst the beautiful art decorating the space. Approaching, you find a simple wooden table with three objects resting upon it: a wooden ladle, a large silver candlestick holding a partially burned candle, and a golden chalice. There is also space for you to place an offering here. Looking down, you now see your offering held in your hands. You place this upon the altar.

Once this is done, you feel compelled to kneel. There is a cushioned kneeling bench behind you at the base of the platform that supports the altar. You kneel there, clasping your hands together and closing your eyes.

As you do this, you can feel a presence in the room. You want to look, but you stay still, eyes closed. Then you feel a warm, loving energy behind you as a being lightly touches your spine. Your body silently quakes in delight at this touch. You feel a different energy placing a hand on top of your head. Your body quivers silently in bliss at this touch. You gratefully receive the gentle touches of these two beings who are working on your body, awakening certain energy pathways, opening particular chakras, activating your physical body even more. You enjoy this as you are kneeling, hands clasped, eyes closed.

You notice that the light touches of these beings behind you feel otherworldly. When they ask you to stand, you open your eyes and see that they are two angelic beings. Thanking them with your eyes for their attention to you, you arise, and they each take one of your hands. The three of you then stand facing the altar. Feeling them pressing gently into your hands, you notice a distinct difference in the quality of each angel's energy. You close your eyes again to take in these sweet energies even more deeply.

After a moment, you open your eyes and see the physical presence of a tall, masculine angel standing before you on the other side of the altar. Simultaneously, the ladle, candle, and chalice on the altar illuminate.

The angel bows to you, honoring you deeply. You feel this honor move through your body in a warm wave, upward pulses of energy in motion. The two angels at your sides release your hands and disappear somewhere behind you. The large angel before you looks into your eyes, reading your book of life, and you feel calm, held in the sweetest love. It is a way of looking into another's eyes that you have never known before, for normally there might be some awkwardness or nervousness, but in this moment, you feel nothing but peace and love. You realize it is a gift you are being given, and your eyes cannot look away — nor would they want to, it is so good.

You hear the angel speaking, though you do not see his lips move. The voice fills your head with sound, as if he were speaking out loud, and you blink a few times as you try to make sense of this. It is your first experience with true telepathy, and you now *know* this and revel in every second of it.

Welcome.

He greets you.

> Initiation One has begun. Feel the gratitude from the heavenly hosts as we welcome your light here that blesses each one of us. Feel your presence here touching all that is. Feel into the fullness that you are, the grand size of you that extends far beyond this holy temple.
>
> Initiation One is to know You, to gain awareness of the vastness of who you are, the many places your energy reaches, your motions touch, your actions affect, your feelings extend. The Angel of Glory has touched your spine, and the Angel of Affection has touched your crown. They have amplified not your energy, but your awareness of your own energy fields. The energy fields are present as you enter Earth as a human being. Your awareness has been expanded to be able to see more of who you are, to Know You.
>
> I am the Angel of the Anointing, and I invite you to approach the altar.

You step forward over the kneeling bench and onto the platform that supports the altar. You now stand at the edge of the altar, directly across from the angel.

He picks up the ladle.

> *Starlight, Waterlight, Great Light, fill my bowl.*

He dips the ladle into a large stone bowl positioned off to one side, and golden liquid light drips from it as he pulls it out. Leaning forward, he gently pours it over your head. Surprisingly thick, the liquid light slowly drips down the sides of your head. As it flows over your ears, you feel a gentle warmth that you have never known before, and you feel simultaneously safe and empowered. You surrender to the feeling of the warmth dripping down, and then you hear the angel speaking.

Anointed. Proclaimed. Present. You Are.

Here you stand before us, witnessed by thousands of angelic hosts above, and we anoint you as present. We proclaim you as here. We see you. You Are.

And You are unique in your inner gifts that were set before you entered the womb of your mother. You have always had them and can trust them as they arise. Delight in noticing their presence when they come up in life moments. Celebrate when you discover a new one, or remember an old one.

Your gifts are your divine path, a blueprint set within you. Your gifts are your guides, your stepping-stones. Your gifts are paired with desires, wants, and feelings of direction, of purpose, and of yearning. Trust the yearning, for this is a feeling that can only come from deep within.

When yearning is present, know that your divine blueprint is activated to guide you ever more into alignment with your path most high. The path most high is the track to awakening, to returning to your Great Self, and it may move more swiftly, flow more easily than other paths. We often call it The Way, and the desire to walk The Way may feel strong within you.

"How do you walk The Way?" you may ask. It is guided by the gifts within you—the things that come naturally and easily to you. It is guided by the yearning within you, the Desires that arise within you.

When we speak of Desires, let it be known that we mean Soul Desires, those that arise from deep inside you as if bubbling up, something that you can "lose yourself" in, even as if overtaking your feelings and mind and body when they surface. Yes, there are everyday desires too that are more temporary, more fleeting, things such as, "I want a nice teapot", or "I want to go for a jog". But we speak here of Soul Desires.

A Soul Desire is for example, "I want to create a work of art that captures the beauty I feel right now in looking at this gorgeous landscape; I want to remember who I truly am." Feel the difference.

Your callings are your guide stones. Allow them! Celebrate them! Free them! Share them! And most fun of all, do them! Find your way to them, for this will point you perfectly along The Way.

Receive this light anointing, through the crown and third eye downward, infusing into the body vehicle.

A reminder: at birth, the head is the first to be anointed in the new atmosphere. So, now are you anointed into this new reality realization of this moment, the first moment of the rest of your life—the moment where you choose now from the heart, from the calling, and know fully, easily, that this is The Way to go. This is the best, most delicious, and most delightful path you could possibly take.

And to know this is to live this, and to live this is to teach this to others, for the greatest gift you can give is the act of sharing your Self, and in doing so, liberate others unto their Great Selves.

This is the first step. Now the candle burns!

The candle in the silver candlestick magically illuminates.

You are the light of the world!

Know this.

For every room you enter, every scene you walk into—day, night, indoors, outdoors—know this: your light is touching everything within sight, and beyond sight. As the sun's light penetrates deep within the body, even though you may only notice the skin's reaction, so too does your light penetrate far and wide in every scenario you enter. For fun, play with noticing what your light is doing in the farther reaches of your awareness now!

This initiation is to wake you up to YOU, to shine the spotlight on your Great Self, your holy light, and to illuminate that you are far more than what you may have been told. You extend far beyond the edges of your body. You are vast, tall, wide, deep, and infinite. Yes, and this is why you may find it easy to lose yourself in the cosmic ocean of sound, thought, light, dark, for you are this. You are the light and the dark, the particles and the space, the sound and the thought and the feeling. Feel your vastness now.

The temple illuminates in a flash of white light. You feel your essence moving outward from you, rounding the corners of the altar and the chairs beyond, reaching to the rafters and above! You feel your light move through the walls and into the grass outside, into the trees and up into the stars. How easily you feel this! You also feel yourself deep underground inside the Earth. You feel yourself as Earth, supporting all the mountains and waters, the trees and buildings on your vast body.

Your essence continues to expand, and now you feel yourself encompassing the Earth and the entire solar system. You see the galaxy and all the stars, and tuning in, you can feel the weight and light of any planet you choose. Seeing the suns beyond the sun, the infinite galaxies, you feel them all held within you. You have a multitude within you! All you feel is love, and that you can hold this.

You are this.

You can do this.

You are this.

You love this.

You are this

Suddenly you hear a crystal-clear sound ringing out through the temple, and your vision returns to the space around you. The angel is standing before you, holding the golden chalice, which he has struck to make the beautiful ringing sound. As it fades, he speaks.

> *Filling this chalice with the Water of Life, I invite you to drink.*

The Angel of Glory comes forward to pour crystal-clear water into the chalice. They reverently pass it to you, and you drink it in. The cool, clear liquid flows through you, bathing you from the inside out with clarity and light.

Know that you are within as without. As above, so below. The anointing light for the head, and the clarifying water for the body. Breathe into this knowing as you take a second sip.

Drinking again, you feel this clarity and calm soaking in even deeper.

Know that you are empowered from the inside first. The calm is the signal that you are in your greatest power. Trust the calm. Receive the calm. Breathe into this knowing as you take a third sip.

You take another drink, and the Angel of Affection approaches you to pass the chalice back to the altar table.

The Angel of the Anointing speaks again.

It is finished; Initiation One is complete.

Here, You Are.

You Are Here.

Receive these words as the heavenly hosts invoke your presence.

All around you, a soft and melodious chant is taken up by a multitude of voices, including the three angels in the room:

You Are Here. You Are Here. You Are Here.

Each word feels like the essence of the complete phrase unto itself:

You. Are. Here.

There must be hundreds, thousands of voices reverberating this truth into your body and ears!

You Are Here. Here.

One word sometimes stands out over another, and you hear it totally differently:

You. You. You. Are. Are. Are. Here. Here. Here.

Relaxing more. Receiving more. Smiling more. Opening your heart center more. Releasing more. Clarity. Calm. Strength. You feel this amplifying in your body, in your energy field, in your vastness.

I am.

I Am.

I AM.

I.

Am.

Once again, you feel your hands gently taken by the Angel of Glory and the Angel of Affection as you are guided to turn around and walk back the way you came in. Taking in the sensation of the energy passing through their hands, you feel so safe, so full of love, so grateful for this experience of knowing more of who you truly are. You offer a song of gratitude to all the beings who worked with you today, seen and unseen.

As you reach the door, the angels honor you with their eyes. You offer the same honor in return, then you open the large wooden door and walk out.

Outside, you find yourself back in the beautiful wheel of light, and you walk to the center to meet me.

Beautiful one, welcome. Thank you. I honor you.

You Are.

And we embrace.

Ahom

Initiation Two

Stand with me in the center of the circle. Welcome a deep breath.

Let relaxation wash over your body like a sprinkling of rainfall.

Feel the prickling of minuscule drops dancing over your skin, noticing first the head, face, and shoulders, then the arms, chest, and back.

This water has a discernible quality to it that instantaneously calms and relaxes you.

The sensation of the raindrops takes you to a deeper and deeper state of presence, until you are sure you can begin to distinguish between individual droplets as they simultaneously fall upon you. Exhaling.

And release this image.

Standing together in the center of the wheel, we look towards the TWO point and walk slowly in that direction. As you walk, you see a beautiful, massive golden pyramid rising out of the sand before you. You notice a shadow at the bottom. Getting closer, you see that it's a double door. Standing before it, you take a deep breath, then you firmly push the righthand door and walk through.

Inside the golden pyramid, it is dim, but most certainly lit, though the source of the light is unclear at first. The space feels vast as you take another step inside. You turn around and feel safe to close the door behind you.

Now you are at the mercy of the dim lighting, but quickly your eyes are becoming adjusted. You look around you. A blueish light permeates the dimness, and you are greeted by two small rectangular pools, one to either side of you.

Looking around, you see a window high up on one of the walls, letting in the perfect amount of sunlight that shines down towards the center of the space. In addition to this are candles placed throughout, along with mysterious luminous globes. It is a soft and welcoming space.

Isis.

You hear this word in your inner ear, and you can feel a presence within the pyramid. From amidst the shadows in the distance ahead, a figure emerges, winged, tall, dark, and beautiful. You feel her eyes on you as you take a few more steps forward.

Isis speaks.

> *Please, come forward. It is my great honor and pleasure to have you here on this day for this second initiation.*

You walk forward between the two rectangular pools into the beam of sunlight filtering down from high above. You notice a beautiful altar ahead, centered towards the back wall, adorned with lavish Egyptian materials and figures, and holding symbols of eternal life: a cross with a loop at the top which you recognize as the ankh, Hathor, Horus, a sistrum, and other objects that feel deeply familiar to your body's memory.

You are just becoming aware of a low humming sound, which has been steadily filling the space for a few moments now. You can sense this unearthly sound supports the altar and Isis's presence in a way that lifts their already shining radiance into a new light. The sound is now coming from all around you, and you lift your head to see that a large chorus of women has gathered around the perimeter of the pyramid, robed in white, supporting the initiation with their resonant voices and their high light vibrations.

Tuning into your inner vision frequency, you can see that these sound vibrations are creating a sacred space that allows you to lift even further out of everyday space and time, and whatever transpires within this pyramid will be supported and held by these sound waves of divine and loving light.

You are in awe that so many women would show up to support this initiation, and you become aware that each of them has gone through this ritual as well. You feel so many feelings, from gratitude and pride to unworthiness, and you allow these feelings to be lifted and transmuted by the vibrations sung by all present.

As your awareness returns to Isis and the altar, you notice your body relaxing into the space created by the beautiful sound of the women supporting you. This is your moment, and it is okay to be wholly focused on your own experience now.

Isis speaks.

> *Thank you for relaxing into the sounds of our Hathor chorus. She is with us, as you can feel through the vibrations being created in this space now, and you are supported in every direction you can imagine—and even in some that you cannot.*

She picks up the ankh from the altar and places it in your right hand. It feels heavier than you expected, and immediately you feel an electric energy surging through your hand and into your arm.

> *Behold the ankh of life—the power of the direction of your focus, the aim of your thoughts, the weight of your intention. It is the amplification of your present vibration if this is not yet in your awareness, and the projection of your vibration, intention, and purpose outward upon that which is beyond you.*

You notice it feels so good to hold this sacred object! Your mind feels clear, and all of your attention is focused on the powerful sensation of holding the ankh.

> *Bring the ankh now in front of your heart center, and take hold of the stem with both hands. Envision with me your etheric wings rising out of your back. Allow the ankh to help you with this vision. Feel how easily your wings unfold from*

their origin just beneath your shoulder blades and begin to stretch outward.

Isis does the same with her own wings, providing a visual imprint for your eyes to follow.

Breathe calmly and remain centered as you feel the wings unfolding from your back, assisting them by relaxing more into the power of the ankh.

You notice it is easy to feel your wings emerge and unfold fully once you lean into the power of the ankh. The women continue to sing softly, humming and oohing behind you.

This is it!

Isis exclaims.

Feel the fullness of your outward expression, from heart center to wing tip, from your palms on the ankh to the parts of your energy field touching the outer walls of this pyramid. Initiation Two is your Initiation of Space: taking up the space that you are, working with the space around you and within you, and knowing when to be big and when to be small.

This Initiation of Space will empower you to move through your life easily, as if you are commanding your reality to adjust to your intentions, needs, and desires. Space is a continuum, just like time; it is more flexible than we often realize. Working with this flexibility easily is one outcome of this initiation.

As she is speaking, you notice a shift in the energy behind you. You turn to look, and all the women have their wings fully extended, creating the most beautiful sacred geometrical shape against the walls of the pyramid. Isis has her own beautiful wings on full display, and yours are fully extended too. The feeling in the air is one of extreme power and potency. You sense a swirling energy, and see a portal is being created simply by the sheer immensity of the energy that comes from having your wings up and fully outstretched. You feel this energy strongly in your heart center.

Isis speaks.

> *Relax even more deeply into this energy of self-sovereignty, the energy of not holding back any part of you, for the sheer enjoyment of letting all that you are, the immensity of who you are extend outward from your core.*

The song of the chorus undergoes a beautiful shift as they begin singing not words, but sounds of power—light language—and you can tell that these sounds are doing something to the energy in the pyramid. They are amplifying it, moving it. You feel the ankh warming in your hands. It is responding to these new frequencies.

Isis instructs you,

> *Turn now to face the singers!*

You turn to receive these vibrations directly into your being. It is incredibly powerful.

> *Extend the ankh of life!*

With arms outstretched, you wield the ankh before you and feel even more energy moving through your body. As if you are a musical instrument, the ankh is an amplifier, moving your vibration up, around and out, wider and wider throughout the pyramid. You feel your energy reaching up to the top, not gently but powerfully, like a sweeping tide rising.

As you hold the ankh at the level of your heart, you can feel your heart energy passing directly through the center of the ankh and becoming more active and tangible, differentiated from the rest of your energy, working now with all the energy vibrating off your body—like your heart energy has become conscious! It directs your energy upward to intersect with the vibrations of the chorus, forming the most beautiful sacred geometrical shapes. Then you sense it directing your own energy back into your body, coming in through the back of every chakra and shining out again through the heart, amplified by the ankh. Simultaneously, you feel your energy everywhere in this room!

Isis moves to stand before you and touches the center of your forehead. Suddenly the pyramid disappears; the walls and floor fall away, and you are suspended in the blackness of space. All that is around you is your energy. All that is here is your expanded energy, in every direction. You are floating on your energy, held by your energy. In fact, you realize you are this energy! In this vision, you see a subtly golden river of distant stars, barely visible in the blackness, and when you feel into this, you find your energy here too. Above you is endless energy that is yours; below you is endless energy that is yours. You find your way to this river of starlight and float on it for what feels like some time, swirling in the light and the star particles, basking in it for a moment that seems beyond time. Are you in outer space? Or inside a cell in the body? It feels very good to float in all this energy.

You begin to feel a sense of solidness returning as a sound brings you back to the pyramid, wings still extended. A sistrum is being shaken by Isis, and now the women are singing rhythmically and powerfully as she is moving through the room, bringing the high-frequency sound to every corner. One woman with a drum is providing the heartbeat. The women are doing a sacred circle dance that moves them slowly around the perimeter of the great temple. You can feel the energy of this swirling movement, and it makes you want to move your body. There is so much energy here in this giant space!

You begin to move your wings as Isis approaches, takes the ankh from your hands while holding the sistrum in the other, and invites you to move through the space as you are called to move. You walk into the middle of the pyramid, letting your wings guide you and allowing your body to become lost in these vibrations as it moves in every way it feels called to move.

As the song continues to soar, you find yourself standing in the very center point of the pyramid, illuminated by the spotlight of sunbeams shining down through the high window. Noticing how little effort it took for you to keep your wings extended, you stretch them out as far as you can, standing perfectly still as the women and the energy in the room all swirl around you.

There is a noticeable shift in the music, and the ladies pause in place, still singing, stationed in beautiful sacred geometry with their wings out.

Isis speaks.

> *The Initiation of Space is one of self-knowing, in a vaster and broader way than the limits of the physical body. In an instant, we can take up the space of this pyramid, of this galaxy, of a mouse, or of an electron. The Initiation of Space reignites the ancient power of shape-shifting, always through the pure intention of the heart, guided by unconditional love—a most successful way of achieving greater understanding of Self, and execution of divine intention.*
>
> *Know that the space you just experienced outside of yourself is also within yourself. Now, we express the fullness and the power of our vastness as we take up space!*

The women begin to chant a powerful syllabic mantra, and suddenly you feel a strength within you and outside of you that you have never known before. You witness your body moving you around the space in a way you have never moved before. Each step taken by your legs, and each motion made with your arms feels so broad and wide and tall—your vastness. Sensation tingles through your entire being.

Isis speaks.

> *Self-sovereignty is an act of knowing your own vastness, and discerning when to be what size in space. Today you are initiated into this knowing. Today you are empowered to use this gift.*

You continue to move around the room in the way your body calls you to move, until you notice a shift in the music. The chanting women are bringing their voices down to a gentle hum and folding their wings. Holding your right hand, Isis guides you back to the altar. As you face her there, she takes both of your hands, leans forward, and whispers a personal message in your ear.

Isis then adorns you with a beautiful necklace, and the pendant easily slips inside your clothes and falls at your heart. Take in the power of this energy that is now with you.

Isis speaks.

You are the light of the new energy that is to rise on Earth. Trust your timing. Trust who you are. Trust your vastness. And trust your use of Space to bring this new light to Earth now, in the perfect timing. Bless you on your path. I am with you always.

She releases your hands, and again you face the chorus of women who are sustaining a soft low tone. You bow to them, thanking them with your energy and your eyes for their help and beauty.

You hear Isis speaking behind you.

IT is DONE! Initiation Two is yours now.

Go forward in the peace and the light of self-sovereignty, knowing the power of Space is within you. Many blessings and love upon your path!

You are who you hoped you might be! It is witnessed here today!

You Are!

And so it IS!

You walk between the two pools towards the door of the pyramid. Before leaving, you turn to see that the women have receded, and Isis stands by the altar. You bless the room with a flood of gratitude from your heart, then walk through the wooden door on your left to the outside.

I am here to greet you as we walk back to the center of the wheel. I feel your energy and know what you have experienced.

I honor you.

Ahom

Initiation Three

Stand with me at the center of the wheel.
Deepen your breath.

Release the tension in your neck and jaw.
Soften your shoulders.

Allow what feels like a thick, warm liquid to drip from the top of your head, down the sides of your head, over your jaws, softening everything it touches.

Down the back of your head, your neck, onto your shoulders, between your shoulder blades.

Relaxing more.

Softening. Easing into the presence that is the gift of this moment.

Release.

Now we face point number THREE. Here we go in a very direct path, walking together, you and me.

In the distance, you begin to make out something dark and round ahead of you. As it comes into view, you can clearly see that it is the entrance to a cave. Drawing closer, you notice a bubble of blue energy around the space, like a field of loving protection.

As you approach the opening to the cave, you see that it is not grand in size. Tentatively you reach your hand through, noticing a change in temperature inside. You take a deep breath, feeling relaxation wash over you. You welcome this Initiation Three, within this mysterious cave, feeling centered and present.

Now you enter the cave completely and allow your eyes to adjust. There is little to see here, so you venture deeper inside. The light coming through the entrance is enough to illuminate the space before you, and you see a tunnel leading deeper into the cave. It smells earthy, supportive—and did you catch the scent of candles, or is it just the mustiness of the damp air?

The only way to go is down this tunnel, so you begin to follow it. The tunnel is wide enough and high enough so you can easily move through it, the walls and ceiling just out of your arms' reach. The farther you get from the entrance, the darker it becomes, until you can barely make out the walls or floor, but you can still see enough to navigate.

The tunnel runs mostly straight, and the darkness helps you feel the presence of your body in this space as each foot presses down into the rock to propel you forward with each step. It consumes your attention to notice your movement in this way—how easily one step leads to the next step, which leads to the next step, and so on.

Your presence is so fully placed here that at times you wonder if it is really you who is doing the walking. You are able to observe so deeply the act of taking each step that you feel removed from the action and are able to delight in the observation of the process. It is wonderfully meditative.

After a while, you arrive at a very pronounced curve in the tunnel. Your awareness again becomes focused on the space around you, and you continue forward, curving sharply to the left now.

As it straightens out, the tunnel begins to descend in a gentle slope. After a moment, it curves sharply to the right. Soon it turns again to the left... You realize this zigzagging, sloping path is easing you down into the depths of this cave, and you keep going, noticing that the tunnel curves seven times before you arrive at what feels like the bottom of the cave.

Emerging from the tunnel in a small antechamber, you feel the energy shift, and notice the distinct aroma of candle wax. Turning to the right, you enter a larger room and see a sea of lit tea lights, placed precisely in intricate patterns across the floor of the cave hall that you are now entering. They form a clear walkway for you, weaving and winding you through a candle maze. You feel the presence of many beings, but you see no one.

Following this path, you notice you are humming a beautiful melody. Any nervousness or hesitation you may have felt drifts easily up and out of you now. You feel totally safe, and yet very curious as to what you will find here. You are slowly walking this maze that allows you to face many different directions as you find your way deeper into this large hall. You feel light, delighted by the beauty down here.

Humming as you walk, the echo in the cave is so spectacular that you cannot help yourself; you lift your voice in sweet song to rejoice in this moment. It is your favorite moment, diving deeper into who you truly are in a beautiful and loving space, in the most beautiful and sacred place in nature, surrounded by ancient energies, unconditionally loving beings, and beautiful wisdom. You let this feeling of gratitude and bliss pour out of your mouth as song, drifting and reflecting back to you in the magnificent echo of this stone chamber.

Your song comes to a perfect ending just as you emerge at the edge of the sea of candles. Looking before you through an archway, you see another stone chamber. It seems very empty, except for a solitary stone chair with a reclined back. You are drawn to sit in it, so you slowly approach and settle yourself into the perfectly angled seat, leaning back and letting your head rest against the stone.

From this perfect angle, you gaze up at the ceiling of the cave. It appears as if stars are embedded in the stone above you, twinkling like little lights shining down. Looking up higher, directly above the stone chair, you see a shaft that goes all the way up through the earth to the sky, to the open air, and you notice it has become dark outside. A small cloud is passing overhead, brightly lit by the rising moon. What a beautiful scene!

"Wouldn't it be wonderful if the moon passed right over the opening?" you think to yourself. A tendril of fresh air drifts past, invigorating your body with the scent of the clear night. You're not sure what's next, and you are just about to lift your head from the chair when a voice addresses you. The voice is feminine, and full of power.

Remain in the seat. Relax further here, and receive the beauty all around you through your senses. Feel the cool stone. Listen to the silence and the echoes. Smell the candles and the night's freshness. See the twinkle of the cave lights and the luminescence of the skylight above. Taste this scene with all your senses, and know you are here.

"I am Here," you say. I am here. I am here.

The voice continues,

This is Initiation Three. Welcome! This is the Cave of Receptivity, where you train in the art of opening to receive, for you cannot receive without an open space in which to receive. This initiation will guide you through a process of deepening your openness to divinely receive.

What is receptivity? Why receptivity?

The flower that cannot absorb water or sunlight withers and dies. The sponge that cannot absorb moisture is ineffective. Life force flows through the receptive body easily, while decay is imminent for the unreceptive body.

Receptivity attracts wisdom, joy, insight, creativity, and superior feelings and thoughts. And the receptive being can give more, for they have more to give.

> *Feel even now your body opening more, receiving the experience of this space, its vibrations, its unique light, its unique sound, its unique energy here.*
>
> *Relaxation is the first step in receptivity. A relaxed body prepares the ground to be open to receive. Relaxation softens the physicality so receptivity can occur. Are you relaxed?*

You're still not sure where the voice is coming from, but you do not lift your head, for it would take you out of the deep relaxation that is easily flowing through you now.

The voice continues,

> *The second step is the opening.*
>
> *Feel this in your body as a stretching, a spreading, yet you do not move. Feel your front falling down to your sides, stretching at the skin and beneath. Feel your energy centers widening, opening, spreading out. As if you were butter melting on a warm slice of bread, this spreading out feeling happens throughout your torso first, then through your limbs and head, and finally your hands and feet. Feel the spreading from the center outwards.*
>
> *Now you are relaxed and wide open. From this place, begin to imagine all the little parts that make the body work, like cells and cell clusters, atoms, and even electrons. Imagine these pricking their ears up, so to speak.*
>
> *Do you feel this energetically?*
>
> *This is step three, the reaching outward with full presence, as in a beckoning.*

> *Use the imagery of little seaweeds or blades of grass, striving upward and outward, striving to receive. Imagine that this is happening in every direction off of your body. From your chest, they are going up and out in front of you, and from your back, they are going down and out behind you. Your body is the Earth, and these microscopic particles are all reaching outward in the fullest receptivity.*

You revel in this unique feeling. Millions of tiny receptors are reaching outward off your body, and you feel more sensation than you have ever known. The sensation is so good, so balancing, so gentle, so luxurious. You allow yourself to fully bask in this stone chair beneath this beautiful window portal to the sky.

The voice proclaims,

> *Now, receive!*

A chorus of voices begins, high and angelic, flowing in what feels like every direction around the room. Is the sound spiraling? No, it is surely going left to right... No, it is surely going front to back... It is everywhere!

There is sound in every direction, so beautiful, and you can feel your body receiving.

The singing continues, and you hear the voice gently begin speaking to you again.

> *You are receiving light codes through these sound frequencies that are storing in the body now for future use.*
>
> *Now we begin the seven activations!*

The angelic chorus swells in support of what is to come.

Activation One. Within these light codes are activations of skills, wisdom, and experiences stored in your soul memory from previous lifetimes, such that when needed in a future moment, they will easily be recalled. Receive this now!

Your whole body pulses at these words, like a wave of electricity surging through you. You notice this physical surge at the end of each of these seven activations.

Activation Two. Within these light codes are activations of your own DNA, such that new levels of strength, immunity, and light are now inside your body structure. This new strength will be part of your natural constitution in future moments. Receive this now!

Activation Three. Within these light codes are activators, keys, and particles of light that serve to open your gifts of vision, spontaneous knowing, and communication with nonphysical dimensions and beings. Receive this now!

Activation Four. Within these light codes is a blueprint of unconditional love that integrates throughout your physical and energetic bodies, which will allow for the easy softening of the heart and the ability to call forth this unconditional love in future moments. Receive this now!

Activation Five. Within these light codes is the memory and knowing of the feeling of oneness, that which you began as and always will be, One with the Source of All. That is the truth of who you are. This is embedding in your memory fields to be more easily known and recalled in future moments. Receive this now!

Activation Six. Within these light codes is the memory of the future of humanity, the direction both humanity and Mother Earth ascend towards now, and your direct and easy knowing of your favorite way to engage as part of this beautiful growth. As you know, your favorite way to engage here is your path and your purpose—all the many favorite ways you know. These will be easy to recall in future moments. Receive this now!

Activation Seven. Within these light codes is the birthing and activation of your New Earth body—a body that receives information from many more faculties than just the five senses, a body that is stronger and lighter than the old Earth body, a body that requires less densities, sensing and serving higher vibrations throughout all. Receive this body of light now!

With this last activation, you feel a full-body jolt, sensing that the energies are all within you, as if by some force of electricity or power!

Through the skylight above, you see in this moment the edge of a bright light. The sounds are swirling around you, your energy is spiraling in many different directions, and you realize it is the full moon crossing over the shaft above you now, tendrils of bright white clouds flowing swiftly past. In seconds, the moon is directly centered over the skylight, and you feel the moonbeams shine down like a sacred spotlight, straight into your center.

> *Receive the light of the full moon, amplifying all the light codes just imprinted into the millions of microscopic parts of your body temple and body field. Receive this amplification to the exact perfection of your vibration in this moment here and now! Ahoooooooooahooooooo.*

The voice that speaks now joins in with the high vocals in a haunting solo, leading with a lower voice, intoning sounds and words that open your heart and body more than you ever knew was possible. You receive. You know the feeling. You feel wide open and expanded and fully valid to receive. You feel full, and yet you open to more!

For the brief moments while the moon is directly overhead, time seems to stop. You feel an infinity of space and spaciousness within you, and an imprinting of this memory into your being to be with you forevermore. You witness the moon moving to the other side of the skylight, and even as it fades from view, you still feel the full power inside your body, all of your little particles dancing, filled by this new light inside you.

You sense someone approaching you, then feel a light touch at the crown of your head. She is now standing behind you, although you do not see anyone. Your whole body tingles, and you close your eyes

as she touches your crown …

then your third eye …

then your throat …

your heart …

>your solar plexus …
>
>your sacral chakra …
>
>and your root chakra…

You open your eyes and see a beautiful angel standing before you, very tall, strong, and feminine.

I am the Angel of Receptivity. Know me by the feeling in your body when you are full to glowing with all that you know you are. And in the absence of this feeling, please call on me. I desire for you to know your fullness and bless this kingdom of the Earth with all that you are. I desire this for all beings of light, and I am here to assist anyone any time they desire to expand in this direction, to know receptivity more deeply.

We thank you for receiving, I and my heavenly hosts. You hear their voices echoing in the room now. Blessings to you as you walk Your Way. You now know the fullness of You; it is within you.

Call forth all that you are, and bless the world with your light on all the paths that you walk. Receive our love, our honor, and our glory into the light of divinity that You Are!

>*You Are!*
>
>*You Are!*
>
>*You Are!*

The angel walks away, pointing to another path for you to exit. The sound of the heavenly voices recedes as you slowly shift to stand up from the reclined stone chair. Walking in the direction the angel pointed, you find a stone staircase of low steps that gently curve upward.

Before ascending, you bow to the space and sing out, "Thank you!", feeling a new level of light and love and enthusiasm float out of you as sound. Beginning to climb the staircase, you notice the new strength and energy within your body, feeling more life. It feels as if you float up the stairs, recalling all that you felt during these last moments.

You reach the top, where a push door lets you out into the entry hall, where you left me at the cave entrance. You walk through, and we are again together.

Welcome.

I feel your fullness; thank you for this blessing.

Let's walk together back to the center.

All is well.

Ahom

Initiation Four

Stand with me in the center of the circle.

Today we welcome Mother Mary and Grandmother Anna to be with us.

It is our greatest love to be with each other, including you, and to be reorienting together all that we Know and all that we Are.

Let us feel our bond, the four of us, now.

We hold hands and stand in a cross, feeling our love for each other and this moment.

We raise our hands up, pulling us closer to each other, and as our hands merge together in the center, your hands end up inside all of our hands, and you can feel our love and care pressing into your hands.

Our crown chakras are activated and open, receiving bright golden-white light.

And our feet chakras are illuminated, pressing into the ground beneath us.

It is the most wonderful feeling of love and peace and gratitude, being together in this closeness.

We let go of this moment, and we walk to number FOUR together.

As you are walking towards the number four, aimed as if we had just been standing on the center point of a clock, you notice your body position quite differentiated from the direction of three, two, and one—a new direction, a new feeling, a new sense in the air, a new perspective.

We walk together. The power of our group enfolds you like a soft and safe cloak of love. You notice feelings of relaxation, and excitement, and gratitude, and much ease.

We approach number four, and you begin to make out its shape. You realize it's a watchtower with a square base, not all that grand in size as far as its footprint, but very tall. The structure is made of gray stone, and the top is castle-like, with peaks and divots along the four walls. We approach the entrance, a small door, wooden and arched, and we smile at you as you push it open and walk inside. We remain outside to honor your initiation.

Once inside, you see it is quite a bit larger than it seemed outside. The square base is easily perceptible in the open floor space, and there is a broad staircase directly ahead. Feeling no rush to ascend the stairs, you pause to take in the space, closing the door behind you. The shaft you stand in goes up very high, with a vaulted ceiling at the top, indicating other floors above. You see a window in the righthand wall, and you notice a dove flying out of it, and back in again. Another open window is directly across from this one on the lefthand wall, and there is one behind you as well. The air inside feels very clean, considering it is dimly lit and slightly damp and cool.

You notice a wooden table beside the entrance that you didn't perceive at first glance. On this table is a lit candle, some paper, a pencil, and a few other candles that are not lit. You feel drawn to make an offering before you walk up the staircase. Approaching the table, you pause to ask your heart what it is you would like to offer to this majestic space now. A song arises from your heart, and you offer to this space the purity of your heart through this song.

Then you offer to this space something you would like to release from your energy field. You do this by writing down on a small piece of paper one thing that you do not desire to carry up the stairs with you, or perhaps nevermore. You easily witness this offering bubbling up from within you and flowing out of the pencil onto the piece of paper.

Now you hold this paper in your hands and bring it to the lit candle. It is sitting in a metal plate etched with beautiful symbols. You know it is safe and perfect to transmute your offering through fire here. First you clasp the paper between your palms. Then you raise it up to your face, where your thumbs can easily touch your lips, and as you do this, you recognize the importance of that which you are releasing, the importance it has had in your life up until now, and you feel deep gratitude for this important aspect of your life.

You exhale this gratitude into your hands between your thumbs, feeling it fully absorbed by the paper.

Inhaling deeply, you feel even more gratitude and exhale your honoring of this aspect into the paper again. You are moved to do this several times, until you feel complete.

When you are finished, you hold the paper by the corner and bring it to the candle flame. It easily ignites, illuminating the space as the force of the oxygen and paper and flame lifts it upwards. It disintegrates into invisible energy. Gone!

Finally, as you complete your offering, you see the unlit candles and notice a lighting stick lying beside them. Returning to your heart, you inwardly ask for an intention, a love light desire, to bubble up from the spring within you. This may feel like a calling, a yearning of the sweetest fragrance, emerging within you. As this desire arises, you notice it feels like a spark has ignited in your heart. You take the lighting stick and light it in the fire of the candle of transformation.

With full awareness of this spark of calling within your heart, you bring the lighting stick to the unlit candle of your choice and ignite the wick. As it illuminates, notice how the space in the watchtower becomes brighter. Notice the spark in your heart growing into a flame.

You blow out the lighting stick and set it back down on the altar as you take three breaths, keeping your eyes on this flame of your desire.

Be with your intention.

Leaving your candle illuminated, you bring your hands to prayer position and give a deep honoring bow to the offering table.

You now turn to face the stairway and feel easily and magnetically drawn to it. As you ascend the stairs, you feel them wide and soft under your feet. Although made of stone, there are slight depressions in the middle of each stair, as if many feet have worn them down over time. Your body feels light and easily moves upward on this staircase.

You walk up the first several stairs, and then the staircase turns to the left. After several more, it turns to the left again. It goes up and up, following the contours of the square staircase shaft, and you climb and climb. On occasion, on the wall opposite the tower door, there is a small open window, and you can see that you are gaining greater height each time you come again to a window. The fresh air greets you every time, tantalizing your nose and filling your chest with new life, new perspective, and the energy of laughter.

Finally, you come to a landing. You must now be directly above the tall entry chamber you stood in only minutes ago. Surprisingly, the ceiling here is rather high, and it feels spacious, even though there are more stairs leading up beyond this space. Here there are windows on three walls, and you allow yourself the perspective of these three windows.

When this feels complete, you continue upward, finding the fourth window on the wall of the next staircase. This staircase is slightly narrower than the last, but still easy to ascend. You enter the staircase with the window on your left, then it turns to the right. After a few stairs, to the right again … and again, following this square in the opposite direction from the staircase below.

After a few rounds of walking upward in this way, passing by another nest of doves, you arrive at the top floor. There is no ceiling, just the grandeur of the open sky above. In every direction is a perfect view into the distance.

What a watchtower! It can be seen by many, and from it, one can see very far. Up here the wind is slightly stronger, punctuated by the occasional cooing of the doves, some of which soar in and out of this space. It feels fresh, invigorating, and very clean and clear.

I am here!

You turn around and see me here with you now.

Stand with me in the center.

From the center, we can see less, as we see more of the periphery of the structure, and yet we can see simultaneously in all directions. You notice it feels like a powerful and centered point.

This is Initiation Four, and it is the Initiation of Perspective. Walk with me to the North.

From here you can see in the direction of North, very far and very easily. Take in North!

I lightly touch your third eye.

> *Now perceive North as the direction you're going in your life. See the spark, the desire of your lit candle down at the bottom of this watchtower. Feel your desire fully in your body, and notice that feeling clear and strong. North: the direction of our hopes, dreams, visions, and inspired calling. Breathe in the wind of the north now.*

We breathe in the wind from the North.

> *Now walk with me back to the center.*

As we reach the center, I take both of your hands.

> *Close your eyes to receive.*

A breeze flows through, and after a moment you open your eyes to see Grandmother Anna standing before you. She walks you in the direction of the East, holding your hand. It is so gentle, her grasp, and so loving.

> *Behold the East! Looking out to the East, receive the new light brought in with the rising sun every day, the inspiration and knowing to guide you to the vision you hold at North. East: the direction of our guiding light, inspiration, and creativity. Breathe in the wind of the East now.*

You both face outward to the East and breathe in the fresh air. You feel your body filling up with creativity, guidance, and the light of inspiration for all that you desire.

> *Now walk with me back to the center.*

She takes your hands once you reach the center and says,

> *Close your eyes to receive!*

You feel the light of the sun dancing directly into your body, carrying in its beautiful rays the light of inspiration and creativity. You can feel it going deeply into your cells and infusing you with a sensation of clarity, and access to creative thinking in service of your vision.

When you open your eyes, Mother Mary is standing there, holding your hands. It almost takes your breath away to see her sweet face. She gently guides you to walk with her to the South.

> *Beloved South! Beloveds of the South! This is the direction of the ancient ones, the love and lessons and support that are offered to us from those who have walked before us in space-time here on Earth. Our ancestors, our departed loved ones, our ascended family, offer all to us, for their vibrations remain even though their physical bodies are here no more. They stand directly beneath your dream, beneath North, providing support right at your back. Lean into them!*
>
> *South: direction of the wisdom and knowledge gained through accumulated experience on Earth, great support for the budding visions of the new day. Breathe in the wind of the South now!*

You both take in the wind. And after several breaths and wonderful, loving eye contact with Mother Mary, you walk back to the center, hand in hand.

> *Close your eyes to receive.*

You feel the energies of the loving ancestors, their wisdom and learning swirling into your being in direct support of your vision and desire.

When you open your eyes, there is an empty space before you, and no hands in your hands. Then you feel upon your back the gentle touch of all three women.

Let us all walk to the West together.

And we do.

West: direction of hopes and dreams realized, the knowing and the success of a completed dream! As the sun sets, offering the light for deep contemplation and integration of satisfied completion, the energy of this fuels our inner knowing and our access to the knowing of successful endeavors. This is powerful energy that directly supports the growth of your own dream. Breathe in the wind of the West now!

The four of us stand facing West, feeling the fullness of the energy of the successful achievement of completed dreams before us.

We walk back to the center and form again the circle of the cross, holding hands, each of us stationed in the four directions: you in the North, Anna in the East, Mother Mary in the South, and me in the West.

This is the Initiation of Perspective, knowing that in each direction lies support for the vision, the intention, the calling that bubbles up within us in any moment, in every moment. The full embracing of this support allows the dream to run its course, from inspiration to wisdom to action to completion, evolving in inspiration as it flows. Never doubt this support. These four directions are ways to call on this support for the holy desire that arises within you. For this desire is DIVINE, of our Source Creator, to know Itself MORE through You. Divine you, divine desires; one and the same are these.

When you feel the desire may be too big, too "far off," or perhaps even impossible to achieve, come to the watchtower. Know that here you can gain not only perspective, but support, for true perspective is fully supported, and feeling full support offers new perspective.

Go to the North for clarity on the desire.

Go to the East for inspiration, creativity, and new light.

Go to the South for support from the ancients.

Go to the West for the high light energy of dreams successfully completed.

Perhaps you need only go to one direction for the support you need in any moment. Make an offering to that direction, and be with it for the amount of time that feels correct. You have support from EVERY DIRECTION, the support of perspective. Allow the watchtower to be your platform of support in this most beautiful revealing and creating of the dream that bubbles up within you, your spark of creation! May it be birthed to completion and bless all future ideas in this most sacred cycle of creation of which we are each a profound part! Many blessings to us all.

We raise our hands.

And many shouts of gratitude to the Great One, the great All, for this blissful and beautiful magic of support and perspective. May we all remember we are One, and may we each remember we are ALL. Heavenly blessings to us as we complete this ceremony! AHOOOHHHHMMM!

We close our eyes. When we open them, you and I are standing again in the center of the circle of the wheel.

Feeling centered, we bow to each other.

It is.

Ahom

Initiation Five

Stand with me in the center of our wheel of initiations and hold my hands.

Close your eyes and center in this center of the circle and the center of your heart.

Relax even more here than you have ever done before, as you turn and face the direction of Initiation Five.

Beautiful!

Even now, the heart opens more.

We walk in the direction of number FIVE, and before us the pathway begins to turn into grass, a few blades here and there soon changing to a lovely grass path beneath our feet.

As we approach, we come to stand before the most glorious garden, spreading out before us as far as our eyes can see in every direction. There is an entryway made of wood with beautiful vines growing up the sides and across the top, green everywhere, making a holy living doorway. You walk inside.

Immediately the environment changes around you. All other sounds fall away, and you only hear the quiet of an impeccable and most beautifully landscaped garden. A bird sings in the distance, a light breeze blows through an ornamental tree across the way, the scent of exotic flowers fills the air, and is that the distant sound of water? Your senses are stimulated to the maximum, and you pause here for a moment to take everything in. You see the vibrant colors of flowers in every direction, butterflies and grandiose dragonflies soaring by with buzzing wings as they dip close. You feel the soft grass under your feet, and the feeling of living energy in every microscopic particle of air around you. Sunlight illuminates the colors of each plant even more fully, and your heart shines brightly in gratitude. Truly, there is nothing but love here.

You feel drawn to walk deeper into the garden, down the grass path that leads between tall hedges, creating a living corridor. When you emerge, you see a very large and beautiful labyrinth made from perfectly pruned shrubbery, with pebbles covering the pathway. The labyrinth invites you to enter. The shrubbery is no taller than a foot or so, and you can see that the shape of the labyrinth seems more or less circular from where you stand. It appears to roll out in a beautiful spiral-like shape, and you know this is where you will walk.

On the ground at the entrance of the labyrinth is a rectangular stone slab. This marks the entry point at which the labyrinth will begin its work on you. You feel compelled to dedicate your labyrinth walk, and pause to contemplate what your dedication will be.

When you are clear on your dedication, you say it out loud: "I dedicate this walk of the labyrinth to _____."

You hear a chorus of birdsong in the sky above you as if they acknowledge your proclamation. A light breeze caresses you gently from behind, and you feel the labyrinth inviting you in. Is it living? It is almost as if you can feel it breathing.

You begin the maze, following in one direction, and after several steps, you are turned completely in the opposite direction, winding ever inward towards the center of this large and beautiful creation. You feel a presence — a spirit, a guide — and at your next turn, you see a large angel standing before you. At first you think it's a statue, but then you realize it's breathing, and welcoming you in its direction. It is quite a bit taller than you, strong, and very balanced in feminine and masculine energies. In one moment, you are sure it's a woman, and in the next, you are sure it's a man. You relax into the knowing of the perfection of this great being, and the delight of not needing to evaluate it any further.

The angel speaks.

I am the Angel of the Walk. The walk is the path you choose to walk in your life, and on this day, you choose the path of this labyrinth. I will escort you a ways through the labyrinth, as we uncover the treasures lying within this garden of Initiation Five: Alignment.

The Angel of the Walk takes your hand and walks with you on the beautiful path for several steps. You pause at the next turn. The birds sing wildly. Clearly a flock has stopped in for a visit to this beautiful place.

In life, there are turns in every direction, the angel says. One moment, you feel you are heading one way, and in another moment, things change, often unexpectedly, and you are heading in a direction that may feel like you're moving backwards. As you notice here in this labyrinth, you feel the body turning what seems like 180 degrees, but it isn't quite. You know this is still the direction of forward. You know this is the direction of your path.

Welcome to Initiation Five, where we learn to welcome the inner strength of knowing we are aligned with our divine walk, regardless of how backwards or forwards it may look.

Feel in your body, as you make this next turn of 180 degrees, the feeling of that deep inner knowing that you are certainly still moving in the right direction.

The angel lets go of your hand as you make the turn and feel in your body that even though you're now facing the same direction you came from, there is a difference, only slightly, in where you are heading. It is to a minor degree, yet major, for you know that continuing in this direction will take you to the center of the labyrinth—even though you are now aimed away from it. You feel this feeling in your body as good and strong, with an inner smile to go along with it. You know.

The angel speaks.

We will continue to take many turns before we reach the labyrinth's center. Delight in each of these turns, even as you notice that the direction you are now walking feels like the opposite of the way to go.

Time and experience both align to bring change, shifts in perspective, in direction. There is no way that a new experience, even when it feels similar to an old one, can be anything less than progress. For the new experience, even though it may feel like "We're back here again?", is met by the new you of the present moment, who now has obtained a wealth of other experiences since the last time you cycled through this type of experience.

Presence to this can make these times seem much easier. Presence to this can allow for expansion of vision and even empowerment through these seemingly repeated experiences. Presence to the knowing that the labyrinth must guide you here and back again, for that is the nature of the experience itself, becomes a delight when viewed from this particular perspective.

Truly, the lifetime of a human being on Earth is nothing more than a labyrinth itself, winding and flowing exactly perfectly as it is set up in the rich garden of your life experiences. Sometimes a bird's-eye view is all that is necessary to truly see how far we have come.

Just then, a very unusual feeling comes from above. It is a breeze accompanied by a strong sound. You see a shadow pass over the labyrinth. In seconds, a large bird more beautiful than any you have ever seen lands on the pathway just feet in front of the angel and you. Its feathers are blue in one light and gold in another, with red and green and deep purple mixed in, all shimmering from different angles of the curvature of its body and the rays of the sun. You feel as if your heart stops for a moment as you gaze upon this spectacularly beautiful creature.

> *The Phoenix!* the angel proclaims. *Rising from the ashes, as the legend goes, flying again and again, to know the truth of the perfectly unfolding path. You are invited to gain a glimpse of a bird's-eye view through our friend the Phoenix now.*

The Phoenix speaks.

> *Yes, star child, I welcome you to mount on my back and ride with me to a higher perspective of the Labyrinth of Life in this garden of dreams before you. See the silken wrap I wear? This will secure you to my body as we take flight.*

The magnificent bird bends down, and you see a beautiful blue silk harness that will perfectly hold you close to the bird's back, much like an indigenous woman would strap her baby to her back. You climb on easily, and glancing at the angel, you see love and confidence in their eyes as they give you a comforting nod.

You lift off! To your delight, the takeoff is easy. Soaring upward with a few strong wingbeats, you are instantly fairly high above the garden, and when the Phoenix turns, you can easily see the labyrinth that you were just standing in. You marvel at how beautiful the shape of it is when seen from above, how gorgeously it is surrounded by vibrant flowers and life-filled trees and plants of all kinds. As you fly higher, you can see there is more to this garden. The labyrinth is the heart, even making the shape of a heart, which you hadn't noticed while inside it, and from above, you can see how the labyrinth is an integral part of the whole garden, and the surrounding garden is an integral part of the labyrinth. You see how they support each other in a living symbiosis.

The Phoenix speaks.

> *You see, from within the middle, you can't see where you are. And in many of the turns and cycles, it seems the same as where you just were—doing the same thing, again. Yet can you see how the flow of the labyrinth is steadily taking you inward, in its roundabout way, to the heart of all that it is?*
>
> *So too is the journey of life, every circumstance guiding you as a gift from the highest Wise One to your greatest growth. There is no other way, for even if you do not believe it to be so, what you are draws more of what you are to you. It has been said that what you put out is what you get back. Vibrationally speaking, it is literally happening in every moment, with the exciting addition of the Truth here: each thing happening in your life moments and cycles is perfectly chosen by your own vibration to be that which most supports your greatest growth on this soul journey that you choose now.*
>
> *See where the angel stands as a marker of where you were, but look where you started, and see where you will end up. Each turn of the labyrinth takes you deeper into the heart of the garden, deeper into the heart of all, for your greatest growth*

and expansion of understanding. With this view, you can begin now to trust every moment, for every circumstance happening in your life in any given moment is the perfect one for you now. There is a beautiful gem, a treasure in each moment presented in reality, for you are given the opportunity to expand here, to climb up a rung on the ladder of consciousness, for the great and wonderful delight of ascending to your greatest glory and light of the truth of your Being and Beingness. What a joy and a glory to participate in this delightful labyrinth of alignment and ultimate enlightenment!

In that moment, a flash of light shoots across the garden, dazzling your eyes and washing a white light over both the bird and you! You feel your whole body tingling with delight at the sensation of riding a giant bird through the air, and at the delight of hearing these words that so deeply feel like truth in your body, as you are flying over this garden of dreams, looking at the heart of it all, the beautiful labyrinth.

For fun, the Phoenix asks you if you want to do a circle around the garden. Your heart replies yes, and you fly so fast and so far! The garden is vast with so many beautiful features—ponds, rivers, trees of all kinds, animals of all kinds, lakes, even mountains on one end, and a waterfall! The feeling of soaring upon this great bird fills you with whole-body bliss and delight, freedom and lightness. The garden you witness below you is more beautiful than any you have ever seen, and you feel like a deep thirst has been quenched as you receive all this natural beauty flooding into your system. The whole experience is a rush of the greatest pleasure.

In one large, winding circle, you return to the labyrinth, gently landing on the path where the angel is standing.

Welcome back! And has your perspective enhanced your inner knowing of the way of the cycles of growth and expansion?

The radiance upon your face answers the question, as you still feel the exhilaration of the speed and freedom of flying through the garden. You thank the Phoenix, and he bends to receive your embrace, hugging you back with his head against your neck. Your hearts energetically connect.

Then the Phoenix says,

Call on me any time you need to get a higher perspective, and a reminder that all that is here for you now are gifts of the highest form, serving your greatest freedom and expansion, now and forevermore!

With that, he flaps his wings, lifts lightly out of the garden, and soars off into the sky, with a bevy of smaller birds following behind.

The angel speaks.

Let us continue through to the center of the labyrinth together. I will walk just behind you as you contemplate the turns and the flow, remembering the dedication you set at the beginning before you entered, and allowing the resets at each seeming 180-degree turn to remind you that all is in perfect flow regarding your desires and your present moment.

Together you flow through the labyrinth, and in a short while, you are both standing at the final curve before entering the heart of the great heart.

The angel speaks.

> *Pause here and reflect on all you have seen today: walking in one direction, only to be turned around in the opposite direction, yet ultimately arriving exactly where you want to be, as well as the bird's-eye view, seeing how direction becomes less important when one is perfectly in place and in time.*
>
> *Now bring into your heart your dedication, the one you spoke out loud before entering the labyrinth. Before you cross into the center, survey your own heart for its depth of devotion to this dedication. Once you feel centered in this, step into the heart of hearts, and allow yourself to do exactly what feels correct.*

You take a moment to deeply feel your dedication, then step into the center of the labyrinth.

Instantly, you are pulled down to your knees. You flow with gravity here and press your hands into the soft grass as you kneel. Then you feel a very loving and supportive energy rising up from the Earth to meet you. You feel drawn to pour all of yourself into Mother Earth in the name of your dedication. You surrender to her, and you surrender any lingering force or effort as your forehead comes to meet the ground between your hands.

You hear Mother Earth speak.

> *I gratefully receive your surrendering here, Bringer of Light, to the center of the garden of dreams. When you release in this way, all that you let go of nourishes me as the sweetest food. Then I can more easily and noticeably support you, in all the many ways within my capabilities, and you nourish me, giving me more strength to do so. It is a cycle here too. I*

> *thank you deeply for all that you offer me now and ask you to survey yourself for anything else you may wish to discard, offer, or release into me in this great surrender. I support you. You are safe here.*

You allow anything else coming to mind to be released, breathing it out into the Earth beneath you. You feel a receptivity like you've never noticed before in the Earth, a softness, an openness to your releasing energy, your surrender.

Mother Earth speaks.

> *Now picture your dedication and feel it in your body as an ever-increasing light, beginning in your own heart and seeping outward as it grows in brightness and strength.*

Easily you feel a warmth in your heart around your dedication, and you feel it going outward from your heart and nourishing every cell and organ in your whole being, until you feel you are completely glowing! You feel an energy coming up through the Earth, enhancing this feeling, while you begin to naturally sit up and come to your feet, as if lifted by this energy and support.

The angel approaches to stand behind you.

> *Now know the truth of the heart of hearts, that there is only a gift in whatever presents itself to you in every moment of your life. Acceptance of this gift provides great liberation and empowerment, allowing you to more easily deepen your dedication to your own alignment, both within yourself and with your life's walk, further blessing the Earth beneath you, and all living things. Welcome to the perspective of Initiation Five: Alignment.*

Taking your time, you exit the center, and you have the joy of walking out of the labyrinth the way you came in, with the angel sharing about some of the beautiful plants and flowers growing there, even about some of the birdsong you hear in the distance. You feel light in your body and full of gratitude. You are aware of how good it feels to accept the present moment as a gift, and you feel fueled with motivation to remember this truth in future present moments.

Finally, you reach the rectangular slab of rock marking the entrance and exit of this beautiful labyrinth, and before you part, you and the Angel of the Walk embrace.

Stepping over the slab, you find yourself standing in the center of the wheel, looking into my eyes, feeling full.

Thank you.

Thank you.

Thank you!

Ahom

Initiation Six

We are here! Ahom! We are here together!

Stand again with me in the center of the circle!

Hold my hands, and let's bring our heads together in relaxed connection with the bodies and the energies that We Are now.

Feel our heads, hearts, throats, and crowns all connecting easily here.

Feel the solar plexus, the sacral, and even the root through the tailbone and the legs connecting here.

Feel the Earth cycling her energies, involving herself in our electric connection, and feel the cosmic energies above involving themselves in our electric connection.

We are truly energetically one with everything present here, which makes up everything in existence.

Feel this now!

ELECTRIFYING!!!

Now we face in the direction of Initiation Six. Notice it is a straight pathway, and yet simultaneously you feel a downward sensation as we start to walk there, as if we are walking down to the number SIX as it stands in the lower center of a clock. As we approach, nothing reveals itself to us in our space of empty space. But as you get closer, you see there is a rectangular entryway to a weathered stone staircase leading downward into the ground. There is nothing aboveground, and no sign of any staircase here unless you stumble exactly upon it, as we have.

You approach the first step and begin to descend. There are seven steps down before you reach a landing and turn to the left to descend in the opposite direction, seven more steps. This is the pattern as you descend. One…two…three… four…five…six…seven…and again. The steps are easy to descend, and you notice your body feeling slightly more solid—or is it heavier? There's more of an awareness of the physicality of your body than usual as you descend the steps.

Turning left and left and left, down and down and down you go, and after seven sets of seven steps, you find yourself standing in an empty chamber. It is dark here, but it is easy to see the shape of the room. The floor is a crude stone, and there is a wall to the left and to the right. The third wall ahead is parted by a hallway, illuminated by a different kind of lighting, creating a change in the ambiance.

You approach the hallway, feeling again the density of your physical body and noticing its weight with each step. This comes as an interesting observation, without judgment, just curiously noticing the shift in gravity in this place. As you exit the chamber and enter the hallway, just beyond the righthand wall, the wall falls away, and you are gazing into a gigantic cave. Thousands of feet it extends below you, and several hundred feet above you at the same time. You wonder if you are in a cave or a volcano as you follow the path.

You find that the sense of gravity in your body is actually allowing you to feel safer as you walk this path with this huge open expanse to your right. You remember that every initiation is safe, and you are wholly guided and protected, even as it may seem unusual or a little outside of your comfort zone as you walk onwards.

The wall returns as the path becomes a hallway again, winding you gently to the left, away from the vast open depths. The hallway widens quite a bit, but it is still very easy to see the pathway, and you continue on.

You play with the weight of your right arm, just to see if it's only in your mind that the gravity is different down here, lifting it up and letting it drop to your side. You do the same with your left arm. Something feels different, and you breathe into it, knowing you are safe and all is as it should be now.

The pathway winds back around to the right, narrowing slightly to become a hallway again. And soon you enter a different kind of room. It has a curved ceiling, like an underground space excavated by hand, and in the room is a crystal-clear pool of water. It has a natural oval shape, not very large, and the water is of a different color than you have ever seen in your life. The blue has a whiteness to it, with a pinkish hue in the whiteness, and it contains an unearthly energy that draws you to gaze into it. You marvel at how beautiful it is to look into this clear, translucently lit water — where the light seems to be coming from the water itself! You kneel beside it to take a closer look.

Then you hear a gentle voice say inside your head, *This is the Pool of Past Remembered.* It is my voice, and you can relax into the security of knowing that even though you do not see me or feel me physically with you, I am walking with you every step of the way.

This pool will bring to the surface any feelings that are unresolved, emotions that remain within your being as confusions, that conflict directly with the truth of your divine inner knowing that you are perfectly whole as you are, that you are the spark of God and Goddess living as a human being, that your greatest contribution to all is your Being, and that your Beingness is perfect and holy.

Invite now a moment of the past remembered to reveal itself to you at the surface of the water. You can say aloud in this resonant chamber of stone, "I now call forth a memory of my past that wants to be revealed as a gift of illumination to my true self-knowing here."

Relax your body, soften the muscles in your head, cheeks, face, and jaw, and surrender into the comfort of pure relaxation of the physical body, as you let your eyes gently rest upon the surface of the water.

Deep down, you see something! A spark of light, a bubble… It is coming towards the surface, rising, rising, spreading out as it rises. It begins to take on color, and it is in motion. As it comes to the top, you see it is a life memory, spreading over the surface of the pool. Take as much time as you like to witness this memory.

As soon as you perceive the memory, you notice the emotions that accompany it. Before allowing your mind to evaluate, judge, or survey, just notice where in the body the emotions sit, and offer a comforting touch to these places.

After you physically soothe these parts of your body with your hands, you look back into the pool and notice that the water has returned to its blueish-pink light and is crystal clear once again.

You notice your hands desiring to touch the water. It is okay to do this. You wet your hands with this crystal liquid, then bring your hands to the parts of your body that are feeling the emotion, and touch them with the water. Feel the soothing energies going directly into the parts of the body carrying this emotion. Close your eyes and allow the nourishment to go directly into your body in these areas. Feel loving understanding flow through your hands and the water, seeping directly into the places that hold the emotion.

Once you have finished this nurturing massage, return your gaze to the pool, and ask for an insight, related to the memory that just flashed upon the water's surface. You may say out loud, "I call forth an insight related to this memory, to illuminate my greater understanding of my true Self here."

Gazing with relaxed eyes upon the surface of the water, you begin to see a small light deep below. Like a tiny bubble, it is rising, even swirling, expanding in its unique glow as it climbs higher and higher towards the surface. It carries its own energy, color, feel, and sense, and even before it fully illuminates itself to you, your body is already resonating with the essence of this insight, as if it is already known within you.

In seconds, the insight illuminates on the surface of the water. You see it perfectly, however it presents itself. It is a feeling, a knowing, an understanding, presenting as a vision, a word, another memory, a color, a light wave, a message… Know that however you perceive it is perfect. Take your time here to notice what insight is illuminated before you. Let the vision unfold. It may present itself as gratitude.

You gently return from this illumination, noticing how it has affected your entire being. You scan your body for feelings of emotion still lingering. You ask these emotions to lift themselves out of the body and be held as sacred light in your hands. You find your breath is helpful in ushering the emotions into your hands.

Once you feel the emotions like a gentle glowing globe of light within your two hands, you see them in all their glory. You are able to see them now as light, as their own helpful illuminations for you on your life path. You begin to feel so light and full of gratitude for the emotions that so perfectly guided you to this illumination now. Bending forward, you float them on the crystal-clear water.

For a moment, you see the light of your emotions glowing and resting on the water's surface. And then you witness the water beginning to softly, gently swirl around the light of your emotions. You see that the water is honoring this beautiful light, creating a gentle whirlpool. Is the water doing this, or is it the ball of light from your hands doing this? You feel it is a symbiotic experience, with each playing a part. Eventually, the light of your emotions is taken into the water through the gentlest circular opening in the middle. And the water closes above it. Beneath the surface of the water, you see the light within, in a perfect circle, getting smaller and smaller and smaller, but never quite disappearing.

Then you notice it turns direction and starts coming up towards you again. Slowly it rises to the surface and it begins to take on the shape of what looks like a key. As it gets closer, yes, you can clearly see now, it is a golden key! You reach in and take the key, and press it to your heart knowing it is an important symbol in your own self-knowing. You thank the beautiful water for blessing you in this way, and very easily you stand up, offering a bow of awe and honor to the beautiful pool. You know that this key is yours to keep.

Standing, you see that the hallway continues around the back side of the pool. You take a few deep breaths, feeling the key warming in your hand from your body heat, and place it in your pocket as you take the next steps forward.

You feel different; you notice an easing in your physical body, though you're not totally sure what it is. It is a lightness. The gravity feels less intense now, and you feel your normal body weight again—or even a little lighter. You ponder this as you easily walk down the corridor, which has once again narrowed.

After a few gentle curves, the hallway rounds you into what feels like a viewing room. You enter facing the righthand wall, which here drops to a smaller half wall, and you're able to again see the vastness of the cavern before you. The half wall safely provides a barrier between you and the giant drop, so you walk closer to get a better look.

Deep down beneath you, you can make out what looks like a river, but glowing orange! It truly is a river of fire, liquid magma flowing thousands of feet below. From where you stand, it is comfortably warm but not hot, and you pause to ponder the majesty of this rarely seen power of Mother Earth. Although the sound up here is relatively quiet, given the movement you can make out down there, the scene you're observing carries a type of power that is challenging the edge of your comfort. This is raw power!

After you feel comfortable with the time you've spent here in this viewing chamber, you continue down the path, which begins to descend, gradually sloping. The feeling of density starts to return, the sense of greater gravity here in this place, and you welcome it, knowing it is temporary and must be helpful in some way. You become aware that it has been a long time that you have been down here seemingly alone. The pool certainly felt alive, but you observe that no other beings have visited you here so far.

As the gently sloping pathway curves slightly to the right, then left, winding a little more, you fall into a steady rhythm of step. You wonder, since you are going downward, does this path take you closer to the river of fire?

Finally, after many more steps down the sloping path, you see an arched opening up ahead, and you feel this is it.

When you walk through, a warm wind greets you, blowing swiftly across your face. You peek out, and you are in the cavern of the river of fire! A staircase leads downward to the left, and seeing that this is the only way to go, you begin the descent. It is long and straight, following the rock wall on your left side, which is one of the walls making up this giant chamber. You glance up and all around, feeling very small in this immense space. It is warm but not uncomfortable as you continue walking down.

When you arrive at the small square landing at the bottom, you look up and see a man with a long white beard standing before you.

> *Hello, and welcome to Initiation Six. Here we face the fires and the fears of Any Time. You will find that by driving straight through them, you learn you can outlast and survive anything, and not only that, but you will be shinier because of it. Shinier! Did you hear me? The point of focus is the Shine! Can you do this with me—focus on the Shine?*

You nod yes, wondering what exactly he means.

I am the Guardian of the River of Fire, and I welcome all those who wish to release the heaviness built up in their bodies over time, as from stored confusion of strong feelings, or traumas. I guide people to a new level of self-knowing through the strength to face Any Thing, of Any Time.

As he is speaking, he is working with a thick rope, and you notice a small raft waiting. You are truly at the river of fire now! It is warmer down here than anywhere else, and you notice you are beginning to perspire.

The first step is to take the first step!

The man laughs and invites you onto the raft.

And you may not be used to the temperature down here. So, remember to breathe. Breathing is the most important thing for every moment of intensity that may ever arise. The breath reminds you that you are alive. The breath reminds you that you are present, and the breath reminds the body that it is a sovereign creator.

You focus on your breathing as he unties the raft from the shore. The raft is flat with a foot-high edge around it, and there are two poles on it with little cross bars for you to rest against as you begin your paddle out. The bearded man handles the steering, and you are remembering to breathe, taking it all in.

From down here, the place looks immense! It's bigger than when seen from above, the ceiling impossibly high, with other vast caverns jutting off of the main one.

We are going into the fire, as they say, hee hee! Keep breathing. Initiation Six is to empower you in your inner knowing, firstly that you can make it through all seeming challenges in the Earth Plane, and secondly to give you a deeper understanding of eternal life that is the truth of who you are. Knowing your strength and your eternality greatly affects the outlook you have and the choices you make on Earth. I am the challenger of you to yourself. Can you dare to know Who You Are?!

You feel a whole-body "Yes!" in response to his question. The two of you are now paddling out into a relatively calm river of fire, red and orange, with occasional swirls of bright gold coming up from beneath. You are feeling the intensity, not knowing what it means to go through the fire, feeling very warm, and remembering to keep your attention on your breath.

You marvel at the vastness of this space. It is so big in here—absolutely huge! You feel far away from everything else in this vastness. You notice the heaviness in your body has returned, stronger than before. You breathe. This time, you notice that the weight is accompanied with a feeling of smallness, even hopelessness, regarding yourself.

YOU are the light of the world!

The bearded man speaks as if hearing your thoughts.

Yes, You. You see, the light that you Are is merging with the light of Fire, here in this holy moment! The vastness is purposeful here. We understand the importance of relativity—knowing our size and knowing our depths. In this space, you feel rather small, yes? Perfection! Stay with this feeling, and see if it has any wisdom for you as we journey on.

"Small"? You're feeling small or even closer to nothing in the vastness of this space. You hear in your head sharp thoughts like "I am nothing" and "I don't really matter." Are these old stories surfacing you wonder, or are they real thoughts you're having? You notice that you feel detached from these thoughts, even from the associated feelings, as you continue the breathing—inhale, exhale. "You can do this..." you say to yourself.

The river is picking up its pace, and you are moving into a faster section of it now. The Guardian angles the raft to cross it; he is clearly an expert at this. You relax a little bit more in your body, realizing how tense it has become. You take a purposeful deep breath, noticing you have mostly made your way across. A curve is coming up ahead, and as you round the curve you see a cave. In a moment you realize you are going into the cave!

The cave is small, just wide and tall enough for you and your raft to fit through. Closer now, you see that it is in fact a tunnel, for the other end is near, and the rushing river of fire is passing through it. You feel grateful for the seeming coolness of the cave as the River Guardian aims the raft to go through the tunnel. He pauses while you are inside, where you notice an interesting echo.

> *Receive now the holy rite of the cloak of fire, the all-encompassing flame that transmutes anything brought to it, transforming its matter and returning it to existence anew. And so it is as we go through!*

He pushes hard on the paddle, and the raft propels itself out of the tunnel, entering the rushing river at a point of extreme velocity. He lifts the paddle up, and you are taken by the current, twirled around to face the direction of the fast flow. The two of you fly down the river, bouncing up and down, drifting near rocks but moving away just in time. You realize you have been holding your breath; your entire body is tense, and you are more or less frozen in fear…

The River Guardian speaks.

> *The ride continues, and I offer you the invitation to relax more in the body through deepening your breath. You are in the fastest part now, and you can still breathe! Haha! Welcome in the oxygen!*

You breathe deeply—and then up ahead, you see a rather large fiery waterfall! You feel sure the Guardian knows a way around it, but it doesn't look like you are moving away from it. This waterfall looks like a rain of fire, dropping from a river of fire above and falling directly into the one you are paddling in now. You are not sure what to do, and you turn to the River Guardian.

> *I sense your fear, but there is no need. Just breathe and return to your center, to yourself, who you truly are. You cannot die. You cannot be killed. You cannot be wounded beyond repair; thus is the eternality of your soul.*

You are very close to this fiery waterfall now, and you are feeling the heat and heaviness like never before. You don't know what to do, but you cannot get off the boat, so you brace yourself, gripping the T-bar stand and hoping for the best. Breathe!

As soon as the tip of the small raft touches the waterfall, instantaneously, the raft and you and the Guardian are consumed by the fire in one great flash! But instead of feeling heat and pain, you find yourself totally surrounded by blackness, stillness, and shocking silence.

What happened?

You see nothing, and you feel yourself spread out like the blackness of nothingness. You don't see the River Guardian, but you hear him clearly.

> *You have entered the black hole of your great fear. Being consumed by a fear leads only to seeing what is here, and nothing more. The world around you fades into the truth of the fear at hand, and that is all you see. Fearing death, here we are inside your fear. Relax into the fear, and see what is here for you.*

You feel your body, which is contracted tightly in tension, begin to release, soften, open a little. You breathe. Then you see a distant star in the blackness — a meteor! As it gets closer, you are surprised to see that this shooting star is a picture of a moment in your life. It passes you by with the beauty of a comet.

Then comes another.

And another!

You are suspended beneath a cascade of falling stars, each a moment of your life, playing like a movie reel. One after the next, these pictures fly by you. Although your vision doesn't directly view them all, the body's energy field receives the blessing of each of these memories. They begin to come faster, and you find it easier to see each one more neutrally. Your relaxation is deepening, and you are filling up with a sense of your full Beingness in this moment. You peacefully view the many memories of your life flying by, with a sense of awe, honor, and gratitude.

The blackness begins to break up as you see the waterfall of fire coming into view again. Phrases of empowerment enter your mind: "I dared to do this. I'm in an initiation. I'm going to do this. I am going to receive this raining fire, because I am eternal!"

You willingly ALLOW the fire to rain down on you, feeling the shell of your outer body begin to get harder and harder and harder, while you remain soft inside. It feels like your skin is burning, drying, and hardening. You notice the feeling is neither bad nor good, just unusual. You are now standing under the raining fire, and fully receiving the heavy weight of its pounding—with all the power of your Beingness! As you move through the fire waterfall, you look down at your body, and you see a black crust. It seems that your body has burnt up and become hardened.

You sense you are leaving the waterfall of fire, and you feel thick, frozen, as the River Guardian comes over to you and strongly smacks the shell of your body with the handle of his oar. The blackened crust cracks into pieces and falls at your feet. As it touches the raft, it turns to ash, and you watch as it's blown overboard by a hot wind.

For a split second, you feel a breathlessness; have you actually just lost your body and everything along with it?

But looking down, you catch a glimpse of it and see that your body is still there.

> Breathe.   Breathe.   Breathe.
>
> Breathe.

As the world comes into view, you begin to feel your body again, and you look for the River Guardian. You are still floating on the raft, rounding what appears to be a circle, returning to where you began.

The Guardian speaks.

> *You see, for your fears to be transmuted, they must be in some way active, brought to the surface, so to speak. Initiation Six is the deep dive, down into the cavern, where the river flows as the fire of transmutation for what may be lying dormant in your depths. Notice your body now. How does it feel?*

You notice you feel weightless.

The Guardian continues,

> *Up to the surface to be transmuted. Up and out! Up and out! You were designed for this. Your strong being of light chose this mission to Earth—chose the forgetting, and willingly invited not one, but several great traumas to bear within you, for you to heal them not only for thyself, but for all of humanity! Ha haa! The beauty of the loving heart!*
>
> *And as we sail gently back, notice your heart now. Bring your hands to it, and touch your heart space, lovingly, with honor and gratitude for being willing to take on such an adventure. You are eternal! You just lived through a fire waterfall and*

shed many layers. Notice the lightness in the body! I see it in your field! Hee hee! You have transmuted much this day, Light Being! Bless you, as you have offered much healing to the Great Whole.

In the pause after his last words, you start to feel an incredible peace flowing through your body. It is more than peace; it is peace laced with hope and inspiration and feelings of capability and renewed motivation. You marvel at this, reflecting on such a winding and complex initiation, and release into this new energy.

The Guardian points up, and you can just make out what looks like a bird flying thousands of feet above you in the vast cavern.

The winged one soars again! Not a bird—your guardian angel! Hee hee. You are never alone. You were never alone this whole time. At no time in any place are you ever alone.

Initiation Six: Transmutation by Fire! Welcome the invigoration that comes with facing your fears and surrendering to the transmutation! You have done much for all here today, and we thank you!

At this moment, you are pulling up to the shore, and you realize that along the walls, unseen by you before, are many, many beings of all kinds—hundreds, no thousands, lining the walls in rows, standing on slender walkways going all along the rock, spiraling up and up. You get the clear message that these beings have also experienced this transmutation by fire. This whole time they have been present with you, watching you, honoring you.

> *You can now join them in supporting those who come to transmute by fire the fears that hold the reins within them. You are welcome here any time. Blessings on your journey, dear One. You are a light for all!*

Stepping off the raft, you thank the Guardian, bowing, still feeling lighter than you have ever known in your body — even in your whole imagination. Weightlessness is the best way to describe it!

You turn around to walk back, and I am standing here. I take your hands, and instantaneously we are back in the center of the circle.

Blessings, you wise one. And welcome back.

Ahom

INITIATION SEVEN

Stand with me in the center of the circle. Hold my hands and close your eyes now.

Deepening the peace inside your heart, welcome the vision of a Lamb and a Dove inside the garden of your heart center, white and pure, loving and beautiful.

You feel a new river of love opening, a new channel, flowing straight from the source of love that you are directly into the Lamb and the Dove.

It's a new channel of love, one that you can easily open and allow to flow, and it divides in two to reach the Lamb and the Dove respectively.

Allow yourself to feel this flowing now.

And as you know, tides can turn. Imagine that the current of the river of love changes, with the flow now coming from the Lamb and the Dove into your heart, the core center of your source of love.

Notice the feeling here. Is there a difference?

And let the vision go.

Stand with me now, present in the center of this circle, as we turn to face number SEVEN. We begin walking gently, easily, like we're floating, and feeling very clear. I am just behind you. Let yourself feel the breeze on your face.

Looking far into the distance, what do you see emerging from the field? It is early evening, and the sky is crystal clear, with a crescent moon beautifully illuminating the land below. You begin to make out a tree. The ground has turned to sparse grass beneath your feet, and with each step it becomes a softer and thicker carpet of grass and lichen. You hear crickets gently singing in the distance, and you smell the crispness of the fresh air. As you approach your destination, more and more trees begin to appear, tall fir trees with needles and pine cones. The ground is beautifully clear of any debris as you continue into this gentle wood.

Although night is falling, it is very clear out, and easy to see. There is still a hint of light in the sky as the dusk fades to night, and light shines down from the crescent moon and stars. You walk further into this deep blue light.

Up ahead, you see a very large tree with a sizable knot on the side. As you approach, you wonder, is it in fact a knot ... or is it a door? You smile to yourself, thinking that only a child living in fantasy would wonder if it were a door, or wish it to be one. And you recognize this child inside you.

You are drawn to touch this grandfather tree, and you reach out with your right hand to press your weight into its soft, flaky bark. You glance upward into the myriad branches ascending like a spiral ladder to the distant peak. How many creatures are sustained by this one tree? How much fresh oxygen is given off by this one beautiful being? You thank the tree with a full-body hug, pressing your heart to its trunk and wrapping both arms around it. They do not meet; this is a very large tree!

As you back away from this beautiful being, you have the feeling that you are not alone. Looking around, you see no one, and return to your loving and delighted exploration of this beautiful forest. You glance back at the grandfather tree—and you're sure you see light on its trunk, or was that just a trick of the dim lighting at this time of evening?

Feeling drawn back to this impressive tree, you touch it with both palms. You say, "Thank you for being such a beautiful and great living tree!" When you let your hands fall to your sides, you can just make out imprints of light where you touched the tree.

You rub your eyes; did that really just happen? You walk over to another slightly smaller tree nearby and try again. When you press your hands against its trunk, at first you get nothing. So, you pause, taking in the differences of this tree compared to the previous one. You notice it has a different configuration of branches, with a slight curve in the highest part of the trunk. It also feels different to your hands. It is a fairly large tree, and again you think about how many life forms must be sustained by this tree! You thank it, feeling gratitude welling up as awe in your heart, and you give it a hug. When you back away, you are sure there is a warm glow lingering right where your heart touched the trunk!

Realizing that the sincerity of your feelings affects the brightness of the light imprinted on the tree, you take much joy in expanding into even greater gratitude, awe, and appreciation. You press this love into the tree with your palms, your heart, your arms as you hug its trunk, each time seeing the light imprints more clearly.

How can this be? Is it the lighting in this forest? Is it the nature of these types of trees? Is it that you are radiating light at a new level, more powerfully than ever before? You find a pine cone and try it with this. Thinking of the power in a pine cone to seed a great number of trees, to provide nourishment for animals and humans, and to exist as such a wondrous design of nature, you hold the pine cone in both hands and feel deep awe for this miracle. And when you look at it, you delight in noticing the different levels of light that seem to emanate from the pine cone for a few moments after you remove your hands. You take a seat in the soft, mossy grass carpet to experiment with other pine cones.

RECIPROCITY.

This word suddenly echoes through your head!

RECIPROCITY.

When you hear this voice, you stand up, seeing where your hands have pressed into the ground, leaving perfect handprints in the lichen. Though you wonder where the voice has come from, you are very excited to see that the light imprinting seems to be even brighter in the green forest floor. You give a quick glance around and find no one there, so you bend down to press more love and awe and gratitude into the beautiful earth covering.

You feel filled with appreciation for the beautiful moss, the grass, the soil, and the earth beneath that supports it all, below and around and above you. You feel full-body elation at the idea of how much you appreciate Mother Earth, and you drop to your knees to press your forehead down to the ground just in front of your hands. When you sit up, you see a beautiful triangle of light, formed by the circle from your forehead and two handprints, glowing a gentle golden white in the dark, mossy earth carpet.

Once again, you hear it: RECIPROCITY. The voice is gentle and masculine. You stand up and look around. Who is speaking?

You walk back over to the first tree that you were drawn to, and you suddenly realize this Grandfather Tree is the one communicating with you.

> *Yes, it is me. I am speaking with you now through your very capable telepathic mind. Trees often communicate in this way, for we do not have the same body structures as you do to utilize vibration and tension to make sound. We have other ways to make sound, yes, but these may not register in human understanding.*

Welcome to Initiation Seven: Reciprocity. Nothing you do is unnoticed. Nothing you do can be hidden. In the same light, everything you are is noticed. Everything you are affects everything that is.

You see that demonstrated here in the forest. You are able to witness how your light directly affects whatever you direct it towards. But what you are not seeing is what is happening beyond the scope of your physical vision. Sit here at the base of my trunk, and I will help you see more. Lean the back of your head against me, and relax your vertebrae.

You do this, and instantaneously upon leaning your head back, you are taken to a vision that seems to be of the same place you are right now, only in this vision you are walking around in the forest. It is a replay of the past few moments you have spent here. You remember every detail, and as the vision opens, you begin to see lines of energy flowing out—not only from yourself with every movement you make and every thought you have, but flowing out from every living thing in the scene.

You first take in the living energy connecting each of the trees. You see horizontal lines linking the trees, and vertical lines within each tree, flowing from root to tip. You see how flowing these lines are, gently curving at will. Then you see how the grass and moss interact first with each other, then with the trees. You see the energies contained in a pine cone, and how different that energy appears in an open one compared to a closed one. As you look upwards, you see millions of lines connecting all the needles on a single tree to one another, and also out and across to other needles on other trees.

Your vision expands further to see how between the trees, in what you would normally think of as empty space, there are innumerable energy lines. As your vision zooms in, you see these more clearly as nonlinear, like spirals and swirls, free-flowing lines. In some places, there are little spiral whirlpools, and in others, a more directional flow. You can easily see these in the air, independently of the tree energy lines, because they are of a completely different texture and frequency, and you can adjust your vision at will to view the energies of the air or the communications of the forest.

Your vision expands even further to see other living beings within the forest. You notice a warm glow in a hollow in the base of a tree across from you and receive the information that a mother fox lives there. You look upward to see the glow of animals living up among the branches — larger ones like squirrels and birds, and smaller ones like insects and mice. And then you notice you can adjust your vision to see even the other plants living on the tree, and judging by the interesting shapes of these lines, you sense you are seeing both those plants that are visible to the eye and those that are microscopic!

Your vision goes to the replay of yourself entering the forest and walking over to the slightly smaller tree now across from you. You are stunned to see that every subtle movement you make, every breath you breathe, everything you do has its own energy that exudes into the forest, affecting all the energies flowing through the space. You see how your steps through the soft moss imprint on it energetically, and your energy of curiosity and delight is felt in the ground through your footsteps. You see this energy being received and welcomed by the moss and grass, and the dirt beneath it.

Your vision takes you down a few layers into the earth beneath one of your glowing footsteps, and you see how your light touches the very soil and rocks below, and the living creatures there, all receiving what appears to be nourishment and energy from your single footstep!

You notice how your arms flowing through the air with each step swirl the energy in a unique way, and how your energy is interacting with all around you. You notice a subtle trail of light left by your body as it moves through the space. You see that this trail does not go unnoticed, but is welcomed by the existing lines and swirls of energy in the space between the trees.

You watch as you give the tree a hug, and where you previously noticed the heart light lingering on the tree in your physical vision, now you are able to see what is happening on a broader scale. As you felt appreciation for the tree, the energy from your thoughts and feelings raised the vibration of your entire being, now visible as the light color of your energy field getting even lighter and brighter. It starts out as a yellow gold, then begins to lift to a whiter gold, with flashes of violet and pink in the field around your body. Tuning into the space around your head, you can see the thought waves change from small squiggly lines of yellow to long and exceptionally squiggly lines of iridescent white, violet, and sheer pink. And you notice a very interesting swelling of light around your forehead, along with your heart, both glowing in lightness and brightness.

You adjust your view to focus on the tree as you witness yourself hugging it. You notice the energy of the tree becomes activated; a bright line of light opens up in the trunk, receiving your energy as you hug the tree, while it simultaneously showers down upon you its own bright light energy from its branches above. Marveling at this scene, you can see that the more love you give to the tree, the more it gives to you. The more it receives, the more you receive, both of you lifting and lifting in sublime love and light, one enhancing the other.

Now your awareness returns to yourself sitting against this great Grandfather Tree. Your heart is more open now than ever. Your awe at the miraculous connectivity of the forest, amongst itself and with you, floods through your body, and you look upwards through the branches to make out a few stars and the tip of the moon.

By shifting your focus a bit, you again see energy showering down, this time from the moon and stars. You see how the stars are connected by energy lines to other stars, and to the earth—and also directly with your own body, sitting at the base of this tree. You notice how you can feel these vibrations of starlight entering your body.

You feel an overwhelming love for the stars and their beauty, and you see how this love circles right back through infinite space directly to the star, cycling in beautiful reciprocity, you growing in light as the star grows in light. You do the same with the moon, feeling your heart overflowing with love for the moon's steadfast beauty, and you feel it connecting with your energy field in its love for you, and the reciprocity only increases...

Grandfather Tree speaks.

Yes. Thank you for sharing this vision with me. Trees are blessed with the opportunity to connect with and "see" energy in this way; it is how we communicate.

Initiation Seven: Reciprocity, is to let you begin to see how in all moments of your life, you are connected to and in communication with your surroundings. Everything is alive. Even inanimate man-made things are made of earth substances, and thus in them too, there is life force and vibrational energy.

Connection is the basis upon which everything exists. You cannot separate yourself from this connection that is happening at all times.

As you can imagine, the frequency of your vibration does matter, as to how it is received by the living environment around you. And those times when you are not feeling awe, honor, and appreciation for the world around you, the vibrations continue to go forth from your body into the bodies and energy fields around you. Do not despair, for your light shines no matter what emotion is moving through you, and slower vibrations are rich nourishment for the environment, especially when you consciously direct them to Mother Earth for composting. Welcome all the moods that you experience, for our Mother is always welcoming of fresh compost. And through the acknowledgement of your true feelings, the insight gained can lead to greater and greater capacity for a higher vibration. Yes, welcome always when a mood is less "light" than you would prefer, for there is even greater light to be gained through its honoring and offering.

> *In no time, in no place are you not in communication with all that is around you. See this as lovingly and as beautifully as you possibly can. This does in fact mean that you can communicate nonphysically more than you realize, without words, and without touch.*
>
> *Let's watch you just entering the forest.*

The scene of your entrance returns to view.

> *Can you see here what is happening immediately upon the arrival of your presence? Notice the tops of the trees. Notice the leaves, the needles, the breeze energy. They all bend and bow to you. And your energy is doing the same.*
>
> *This is the truth of your interaction with every scene you experience on Earth, including with other people. The point of the Initiation of Reciprocity is for you to know that this exists, and to delight in it as much as possible—to know the feeling of you being honored and communicated with by everything around you, and to know the delight in honoring and communicating with everything around you.*
>
> *Receive the gift of reciprocity as you stand up and turn to face my trunk now.*

You open your eyes and slowly stand up. The night looks almost the same as in your vision, with quite a few less energy swirls in the air, although some seem to linger in your periphery...

You turn to face the tree and feel him energetically bend forward and place a wreath crown on your head. It is a nonphysical crown, woven of soft young branches from the tree itself, braided and resting easily on your head now, emitting a gentle warmth, feeling very physically present. You are filled with feelings of honor, love, and delight.

The tree speaks.

> *Receive now this knowing that we work together, and we honor you as a steward of the natural world, sensitive to the nature of communication that is happening at every moment in every scenario. Reach out for us with your energy, and we will reach back to you, anytime, every time.*
>
> *We honor you, and we now complete your initiation.*

A strong gust of wind blows through, bringing your body into a noticeably different frequency. The forest looks normal again, and a bit darker, as the moon has slid further down in the sky. But your heart is warm and light, and your crown is tingling with a blissful feeling.

You turn to walk out of the forest, and I am here. We join hands and are immediately standing in the center of the circle.

Blessings to you, light weaver. And what a beautiful crown!

I honor your Initiation of Reciprocity.

Ahom

INITIATION EIGHT

Stand with me in the center of the circle of the Twelve Initiations.

Feel your center point as a small circle of energy within yourself.

Now feel this small circle of energy perfectly centered within the circle of your body's energy field.

Now feel the circle of your body's energy field perfectly centered within the circle of our Twelve Initiations here—three concentric circles in perfect balance.

We can amplify this process by feeling the sun's center point of energy.

Now feel this small circle centered within the energy body of the sun.

Now feel this circle centered within the sun's outer energy circle, the sphere of the reach of its light.

Feel these solar energies coming into perfect alignment within each other, as you feel your own center point come into the center of your energy circle in the center of our circle of initiations.

Find this balance in your body's field.

Feel the three spheres syncing up in a precise balance, concentric circles centered within each other, evenly spaced, poised, and perfect.

Feel this poise even as you are moving, breathing, and walking.

Feeling this together, we aim towards number EIGHT on our wheel and begin to walk in this direction, stepping gently, keeping the poise within our fields. Perfectly lined up with the sun's center, we walk. I am right behind you as you move towards number eight.

Your eyes begin to take in the shape of a dome. It is white at the top, and very large—a full-sized building. As you get closer, you begin to realize that the building itself is cylindrical, capped with a giant dome of smooth white stone. It is so white that it reflects the light like polished white marble, while the walls are a more porous pink stone, perhaps brick.

As you approach the building, you enter a very precisely manicured small garden, perfectly square, with sides delineated by low shrubs, marked by occasional ornamental and fruit-bearing trees scattered throughout. You can clearly see the building through this small square garden, and you have the sense that this garden is honoring you — perhaps cleansing your field as you pass through. Your sensitivities inform you that there is a lot of living energy in this garden, and you can feel your feet and legs stimulated by this. A little bird flies into a tree at the far right corner and sits atop a branch with a small green fruit. The bird's energy feels very high frequency, light, like laughter. Your heart relaxes even more in the delight that your eye caught this bird.

The garden is split into quadrants, and you walk down the middle path. Arriving at the center, you see the crossing path from left to right, ending at the perimeter of the square, allowing the visitor to walk around the perimeter if he or she should choose. You feel drawn to continue straight, yet you pause here in the center of the garden.

There is a concrete bowl of water on a pedestal, large like a bird bath, yet deep like a fountain, still and very pure. It appears that this bowl is cleaned daily to ensure such a crystal-clear effect, and you sense that it is filled with living water. The bowl is a natural gray stone, giving the water a darker color. You note how still and reflective the water is, for there are clouds floating by as clearly in the water as when you look up in the blue sky above. The desire arises to touch this beautiful water, but you hesitate, not wanting to dishonor something so sacred and clean.

Then you notice, just beneath and to the left of this large bowl, a small metal plaque identifying this as Cleanse Water. Below this, the inscription reads:

TOUCH THE WATER WITH THE LIGHT OF YOUR ENERGY THREE TIMES,

BRINGING IT FIRST TO THE THIRD EYE,

SECOND TO THE THROAT,

AND THIRD TO THE HEART.

WHOLLY RECEIVE ITS CLEANSING POWER.

Ahhh! You are delighted, because it was difficult to resist touching this beautiful water. You pause to strengthen your energy field. Remembering centering within the three concentric circles, you feel your center point, within the circle of your body's energy field, within the wider circle of this garden that surrounds you. Simultaneously feeling the centering within the sun, you come into alignment. You sense in your body an illumination that feels like perfect balance, a vertical energy that fills you up like a column of light. Certain that this is the energy the plaque is speaking of, you dip your hand into the still water.

First you bring a few drops of it to your third eye, feeling the coolness drip gently down your forehead. Immediately, you feel an opening, as if your skull has widened and softened, a gentle clearing of your head and thoughts.

Dipping your hand back into the water, you bring a few drops to your neck and touch the very center of your throat. As if the water and your throat are in communication with each other, you feel an instantaneous opening, relaxing, and lengthening of the throat space. It feels gentle and easy.

A third time, you dip your hand a little deeper into the water, and you return it to your heart, touching your bare skin beneath your clothes and feeling the water drip onto your chest. Once again, you immediately feel a widening of this space, an opening that melts throughout your center as a warm liquid light, softening outward from your heart space all over the body, following the course that the blood flows.

Feeling renewed, you bow with your hands in prayer to this beautiful living water. Walking around the left side of the bowl, you continue straight through this garden, taking in the living air, sounds, and feelings of the energy within this sacred square.

Finally, you cross out of the garden and approach the door of the building beyond. The dome itself is slightly larger than the walls of the structure, creating an awning that projects a few feet outward around the perimeter of the building. With your eyes on the arched doorway, you pass through the shadow of this awning. You pull the round metal handle on the right side of the door, and the door swings open with surprising ease, as if it weighs nothing. You imagine the door must have amazing hinges, for it is thick wood and seems like it would be very heavy! Noticing the expansiveness and lightness you feel in your body, you step into the structure.

The first thing you notice are eight windows in a perfect circle high above, around the base of the dome. They give off the most beautiful light, creating a sacred geometry of sunlight streaming in at different angles.

Simultaneously, you notice angelic singing that sounds as if it's coming from the very top of the dome, showering down all around you as invisible droplets of sublime light vibrations. You imagine you can feel this sound landing on your skin as a light rain, and it sends tingles throughout your purified being.

You become aware of the smell of a sweet paraffin wax candle, neutral in tone, but simultaneously conjuring up feelings of holiness and reverence, a feeling you especially love.

The circular room appears fairly empty, for its vast size makes anything within it seem small in comparison to the tall stone walls. The dome itself is white and fairly simple. You walk to the center of the room, noticing that the floor is inlaid with different colored stones in unique patterns. You find them very beautiful, and you wonder what they mean. You walk across them, straight to the center of the room. Remembering the earlier visual of centering in the three circles, you play with this idea, tuning into your body to see how poised you still are in the center of your circles.

Suddenly you notice a voice that stands out among the angelic chorus, a solo of beautiful light language above you. This music is nourishing you through your ears! Along the opposite side of the dome from where you entered, you can see the arched entrance to a staircase hidden inside the walls of the structure.

Up a few levels, your eyes find the soloist standing on a balcony that circles the interior of the dome. She is radiating light in a way that you have never seen before, golden, luminescent in the most literal sense, and the melody she is singing seems to subtly brighten her shine. You feel lost in time as you receive her voice and her light.

Still singing, she turns and disappears into the staircase, her voice echoing down the corridor, and emerges through the archway to walk straight toward you. Though she has no noticeable wings, she is clearly an angelic being; you are sure of this because of the light emitting from her body. You notice she fades from view ever so slightly here and there, and you marvel at her immense beauty. You feel safe, and so loved, with a warm glow in your heart, like the feeling that was initiated at the sacred cleanse bowl in the garden a few moments ago.

Then she shifts into singing words you recognize!

> *Sing to shine your brightest light, Sing to bring your being high,*
>
> *Sing to know your meaning, Sing to let your love light shine.*

She pauses, and the chorus shifts to a calming hummm, a meditative sound.

She speaks.

> *Welcome. I am the Angel of Highest Light. I welcome you to this space of enchantment for your expansion of the light that you are. This is Initiation Eight: The Initiation of Highest Light takes Flight.* She giggles.
>
> *I love to rhyme, in English or in the language of angels. The congruency of vibration when two sound frequencies align in time demonstrates to me the circle of life, the flow of cycles, and the beauty of the truth of the eternality of all that we are.*

> *Take my hands and relax into my energy, so you can feel more present with this space and this moment. Close your eyes and receive.*

Taking your hands, she spins around with you, helping you loosen up your body even more. As you come to a stop, you close your eyes and notice a warm energy flowing very physically from her hands to yours, heating up your hands and gently flowing up your arms and into your shoulders, beginning to spread through the back of your throat and down through your torso. This energy feels like what you might imagine fairy-tale magic feels like, when you visualize a golden light extending from a magic wand, or a healer's hands performing a miracle. You delight in this warm light spreading all over your body as you hold her hands, and it moves through your pelvis and down your legs, warming even the toes of your feet, and now your whole head and the top of your scalp. She lets go of your hands, and you marvel at how golden, light, and glowing you feel!

The angel says.

> *Now to create some high light vibes in this space!*

The chorus of angelic voices steps up in tempo and begins a rhythmic song as one by one they begin to stream down from the staircase into the circular space where the angel and you are standing. They begin prancing, even lightly running in a circle around the perimeter of the dome in a counterclockwise direction. Running, running, they run and sing and seem to never get out of breath, even as their energy is physically changing in the space.

The angel speaks.

Stay in center! Do you see how the motion around you actually creates a feeling of support for you to stand even stronger within the three concentric circles of energy?

The dome fills with sound as the song increases in speed and intensity, rhythms and syllables pulsing wildly through the room. You realize a drum has come in, and you look up to see a woman holding a frame drum in the window of the stairway, its steady drumbeats echoing throughout the circular space.

Now let the music move you!

The angel runs to join the circling women, and you are left in the center. You feel called to first close your eyes and more deeply feel the energy in the room while standing still. You notice how it is interacting with your body and your energy field.

You continue to feel the glowing sensation from touching the angel's hands, and you feel lighter than ever. With eyes closed, you feel the call to begin turning in the opposite direction than the ladies are moving, as the song escalates and the room spins more and more and more. You feel this spinning, and you lose your sense of place. Cracking your eyes open, you re-center, then close them again. You feel a great unwinding, something happening within your body — something ancient being stirred and awakened, something old being shaken up and out.

Suddenly you are filled with the desire to fully receive these energies in a new way, and you feel your body begin to pulse with the rhythm of the music. Opening your eyes, you let the body express through movement all that it knows it must, releasing old energies that have been stirred up by this influx of high light. Ancient knowings, gifts, talents, and skills are wakening in you now, and you want to feel their presence for the first time in this incarnation in your physical body. You let them flow. Moving your body as if someone else is operating you from the inside, you trust your body's movements, you trust your body to know exactly what it wants to do. More like an observer than a dancer, you witness these movements as your body takes you all over the room.

The singers are peaking now in intensity, and you feel called to spin and spin in your own direction, shaking and calling forth all that you are, clearing out all that you no longer need, experiencing a full-body renewal as you shake and spin and move, until finally you release your whole body onto the center point of the floor. Lying on your back, you receive a few moments more of the singing, until the voices quickly come to a calm.

Then ... SILENCE.

In the silence, you are able to notice more easily the energies of the room still spinning wildly around you. The force of the spin is so noticeable, you wonder how many days or weeks it will take for it to slow down again! You feel a responsiveness in the floor, and you remember it sits on Mother Earth's supportive energies and is made of rocks taken directly from her breast. You let this grounding feeling fill you and anchor your place in space as the spinning energy begins to slow down.

Empty.

Clear.

Cleansed

Open.

Reborn.

Rejuvenated.

Alive.

Still.

Where is the center now? As you lie on the floor, you recall the three concentric circles of energy, and you notice they are relatively easy to sense now in the spinning energy.

The angel speaks.

Stay in center.

The singers begin to oooh in a beautiful chorus, supporting all this angel says.

Here in Initiation Eight, you notice the eternity that is the motion of any motion out to infinity. Although the spin will slow in this room soon enough, these vibrations exist now and forever in the universal all. Why project a vibration of density when you could be so light? Feel your body now.

In the stillness of lying on the center of the stone floor, you have the overall sense that you are floating, not noticing the points that bear weight, feeling truly weightless here. You notice the glow warming even the most random of your body parts, like your calves, elbows, ears, and lips. You marvel at the vibration you must be putting off into the world now!

The angel has walked over to you and is singing sweetly over your body. You feel the vibrations enter like a soothing balm rubbed over you. She touches your third eye, and for a split second, you can see the energies that you exude now. Most fascinating of all is the large golden column that extends up and out of your center and up through the center of the dome. The swirling is still happening in this nonphysical vision, and you see the singers have begun a slow dance in the opposite direction of their original spin. The energies are returning to stillness, and your shining is the point around which all is flowing. You realize that if you were to move, the entire balance would be different.

As this vision fades, you sit up. You imagine that this is right where that column of light would have been that you just saw in nonphysical vision, and you feel a unique strength in yourself.

The angel speaks.

> *Rise, strong one! Receive the light of the highest, and feel free to shine this now!*

In this moment as you get to your feet, the angel begins to glow again, even brighter than before. The women in the room continue their meditative singing, and they all start to glow as well. You are now standing in the center of a circle of glowing singers, beside a glowing angelic being. She looks at you with a nod, encouraging you to go into your own full glow.

Beginning in your heart, you feel the centeredness. Then you feel the balance within the three concentric circles. Then you feel the warm light, cleansing and activating, spreading out within you. Then you feel a gentle elation that comes with the expansion of this glow, and you look down at yourself and see that here you are, glowing as the ladies glow, as the angel glows! Your column of light shoots upward simultaneously with the angel's, and your two pillars are perfectly centered within the glowing circle's circumference. Where the circular outlines of your column and her column touch, an infinity sign imprints on the ceiling of the dome.

The angel speaks.

> *Initiation Eight: be the full light that you are, for what you shine out goes on for infinity. You are a powerful creator being, and when you are filled with your light, radiating your bright vibration, you are centered in the support of the light of all. And when you fully shine, your access to the heavens opens!*

She gestures upwards, and for a moment the dome disappears, and you are looking up into the heavens, a sparkling sky of stars. You see your column and hers extending up and beyond, directly receiving energies from many stars, and in one moment directly connected to the center of our sun, receiving and sharing that divine spiritual light.

The angel says,

> *This blessing is for all of us, for when you shine your brightest, the whole world, the whole universe benefits. We know this, and now you know this. This is Initiation Eight, and we honor you.*

The women begin to create a spiral to exit the space, one row folding in front of the other, rotating through the archway and up the staircase, returning to the balcony and closing the ceremony with a final round of angelic singing. The angel bows to you, and you hug each other. She feels so sweet and so familiar. It is natural to embrace here, and both of you receive great light as your hearts come together.

She turns to walk up the staircase as you turn to walk back to the door. The singing gets softer and softer until you cannot hear it anymore as you cross the threshold to the outdoors.

I am waiting for you outside. We walk through the square garden together, and quickly the grounds change back to the empty space, and we are once again in the center of our circle of initiations.

I honor your light.

Ahom

Initiation Nine

And here we are.

Feel a swift counterclockwise whirlwind of light surround your body in a quick spiral upwards, from your ankles to above your head in a whoosh!

You begin to feel this whirlwind pulsing rhythmically now.

Whoosh, whoosh, whoosh, whoosh.

On each downbeat, you feel a strong connection in the base of your spine, a pulse.

Whoosh, whoosh, whoosh.

And you feel a rising rhythmic light pulsing upward along your spine with each whoosh. You feel it definitively in the spinal column, and cresting out of the top of your head, like plumage or a fountain, gently spouting out through your crown.

Whoosh, whoosh, whoosh.

Now let us aim ourselves towards the number NINE. We walk straight to it in the direction that feels like west, you a little in front of me, present with the invigorated spinal column and the tingling in our hands from the increased blood flow.

Looking ahead, you see only emptiness. But it feels good to walk, so you pick up the pace a little, and I am right behind you. It's okay if you see nothing; there is purpose in the walking. Step, step, step… Remember the rhythm of the whoosh, whoosh, whoosh. Feel the effect of each step you take in your whole body.

Step, step, step…

You look ahead and see beautiful hanging gardens, latticework with plants and flowers, ivy and other vines growing down from the planters. Little lights are interspersed throughout the hanging arms of the dripping leaves and vines. This place feels very peaceful and full of magic. It is dusk, so the little lights are easily seen sparkling above you, with longer rope lights wound around the simple wooden columns. There are chairs that recline underneath the hanging gardens, and a bench on the curving perimeter.

Passing through this living patio, you see before you a house, the kind that you might find in Greece or Italy, made of smooth white concrete-like stone, with lights pointing upward at the sides of the house, giving it a yellow cast. The roof is red, deepened to a dark brown in the dusk. Even though it is very quiet, you feel a sense of welcome here. You wonder if you are to go inside the house. Along the right side is a terrace, and you feel drawn to walk this way first before knocking on the door.

Stepping onto the terrace, you realize you are high on a hilltop, and you can see for miles, all the way to a body of water still shimmering silver in the setting sun. Many tiny dots of lights flicker on the distant hillside. What an incredible view! The stars are just beginning to come out, only one or two yet, and the sky is crystal clear. You breathe deeply as a gentle breeze washes over you, reminding you of the feeling of being wholly and deeply at home.

What is home?

You hear these words from behind you, and you turn around to see an older woman walking your way, filled with vitality, with a beautiful multicolored shawl over her shoulders. She has the gentlest energy about her, and a soft, sweet voice with a hint of great wisdom.

The woman speaks.

> *"What is home?" you may ask as you look out and see the many places one could rest their head—the many houses, the many terrains, the many natural spaces, the many depths, heights, latitudes, and longitudes one could call home. Many say home is where they feel safe, comforted by mostly those who bore them, like parents, siblings, neighbors—FAMILIARITY.*

She pronounces it: *FAMILY-arity.*

But many say that where they were born, or with their families, is not where they feel safe or comforted, nor where they belong, and they go searching and searching for their own home. So, is home familiarity? Is home being settled? Is home automatic? Is home merely an unnoticed foundation upon which the rest of our "real life" unfolds? Why are so many on the quest for home? It is said that home is where the heart is. We have it wherever we go, yes? But does this seem ... enough?

Welcome to Initiation Nine: Home. Do we ever get there? "THERE." Is there ever a stopping point?

Perhaps the closest we get is that moment when we are lying in bed at night, wherever this bed may be, or in whoever's "home" it is, and we surrender into the safety of sleep. Yet what truly stops? What does not exhibit change? Though earth, fire, wind, and water are constants on this planet, they are continuously in transformation. You see this with all the elements, constantly changing. Even ancient stones thousands of years old are eroding microscopically in every moment. With constant change being a truth here on the Earth plane, where could home truly be? Where could familiarity and constancy be when all is changing in all moments?

I am going to show you a story.

She removes her shawl, and as she spreads it out on the terrace, you can see it is a tapestry made up of a series of embroidered images.

You see here, Maikai is looking for home. She gets on her horse, she rides off into the sunset, and she begins her journey. Along the way, she encounters wild beasts, untruthful humans, and interesting friends. She finds beauty in little things, like stones and ladybugs, and in big things, like the waterfall and the sun setting over the mountain.

She points out these scenes on her shawl.

But her heart feels empty, though greatly expanded in the moments when she does allow the beauty in.

One day, she finds a beautiful land with a charming town where she feels for the first time that she belongs. She makes friends with the gatekeeper, the bread seller, and the woman who cares for the children, and she feels the call to be here, to open her heart here, and to commit herself and her talents here.

But a dragon has been terrorizing this land, and one day the dragon comes through and burns down practically everything. Some people are badly hurt, and Maikai wants to help however she can. She decides to go address the dragon to try to save these lovely people and their beautiful town.

She sets off from this place, riding into the sunset, and she finds out that the dragon lives inside the mountain, so she heads there. Behind the waterfall, she finds an entrance to a grand cave, and she waits. It is quiet, and the cave is dark. Though the dragon is not here, she knows it will be soon, so she waits. Three days pass as she is waiting there, having finished all the food she brought with her, and as her stomach rumbles, she is taken over by an ugly feeling. What is she doing? She left home, where she didn't fit in, to find a new home, where she felt like she did fit in, but now she is seeking out a dragon—for what? What is she doing?

Finally, the dragon returns. Maikai is terrified, yet she walks into the space where it lives. The dragon, a female, asks her why she is there; she could burn her to pieces instantly. Maikai says she felt like she had finally found her home, but the dragon has just burned up everything, and now she has no home again.

The dragon looks at her with big eyes and sees her folly. Though she is an angry dragon, she is wise. She says to Maikai, "You keep running away from the one thing that will give you the peace you seek—and it is inside you, so you can never be without it."

This rings true for Maikai, who wonders just what it means. "Why are you burning up the people and their homes?" she asks.

"They have taken my egg and I will not stop until it is returned to me. What is home, anyway? Just a place where you lay your head, where you feel safe or loved? I have no love here, with my egg stolen. I have no home here with my egg gone. And yet in this cave I have lived for millennia."

"I will get your egg back, and you can stay here," Maikai says. "You will be at home with your baby, and I will learn something from this about my own home".

So, Maikai returns to the town, and finding the elder, she explains the dragon's situation. He was unaware that the egg had been taken, and together, they soon discover a young warrior who thought he could sell it and had stored it in the basement of a food storage house.

Maikai takes the egg back to the dragon, and the dragon has tears in her eyes as the egg is returned. As she approaches the dragon to hand over the egg, one giant tear falls from the dragon's eye onto Maikai's head.

Immediately Maikai is washed over with an illumination of her own inner sadness, with the recognition that she has not made herself at home in herself. She instantly sees that there are many parts of her that are unwelcome parts of herself. She sees how she has allowed some parts of herself a home in her heart, and other parts she has left out, and a few she has kept far, far away, at a great distance, hoping to forget them completely.

The dragon tells her, "The outcast, or separate one, can only know welcome when brought inside. See now these parts of yourself that you cast out, and call them back home."

So, Maikai looks within herself and sees anger at her mother, hopelessness about her hometown, impatience at herself, fear of being cast out forever, fear of failure, fear of being unlovable, fear of being irreparable. Thanks to the dragon's enchantment, these parts of herself now stand before her as seven lost girls, dejected and true to their feelings (anger is angry, hopelessness is hopeless, and so on).

"The only way home is to invite them in," the dragon tells her. "Invite them into the great receiving hall of your heart. Invite them to sit down on the beautiful furniture, to relax. Welcome them home. Thank them for bringing their unique energy here, to your home. Say to them, 'Welcome home. You can stay as long as you want to.'"

So, these seven cast-out parts of herself walk up a ramp directly into the great hall of Maikai's heart. At first, she is nervous; what will this do to her? But when they get inside, she notices she doesn't feel too different; well, maybe she feels the slightest bit better. Then in her mind's eye, she goes to the center of her heart's great hall, and she addresses the group as the dragon has advised.

"Hello, everyone! Thank you for coming. I want to welcome you here. You can stay here as long as you want. I thank each of you for your unique energy. I honor each of you as individuals, and I have a very large pot of hot tea ready for you, on the cart over there by the wall, should you like to have a cup. Please help yourself."

Maikai can hardly believe she is feeling a little bit better! She asks the dragon if she can stay there for the night, and the dragon welcomes her.

That night, she has an interesting dream. Once again, she is inside the great hall of her heart, and she sees all these parts of herself that she didn't like still sitting around, some drinking tea, others with their feet propped up on the table. In the dream, Maikai is a sorcerer with great powers, and she has a plan to change each of her guests into something better. She is very good at transformations, and she could change each of these parts of herself into something nice, like a flower or a beautiful bird, perhaps.

As she approaches her first guest, Anger, and tries to cast the spell, her powers are halted halfway between her and the guest, so that Anger does not even notice she is trying to transform her. Maikai tries several times, and Anger is simply looking at her, wondering if she is going to say something.

At the peak of her frustration, Maikai speaks. "Why are you here, Anger? I have trouble with the feeling of anger; I don't like to feel it."

Anger says, "I am here because I am part of your loving heart that became confused in a contradiction of your great knowing. I came into creation to make things better for us."

"You are here because you are part of my loving heart?" Maikai thinks to herself.

And in that moment, she sees Anger transform in a flash into a beautifully pure and innocent part of herself, and then back again to the angry vagabond she presents as in the moment. But she can see that beneath the roar and the teeth, there is only love—only love in this pure being that wants to create the best life for her. Her sorceress heart softens in that instant, and Anger is fully transformed into the beautiful version of herself, in a white gown, with a face of peace and calm.

So, Maikai goes to each guest, knowing that forcing them to transform into something else will not work. She asks why each is here. Through their explanations, she sees that at the core of each of these most horrific feelings is love—and each time, the guest is transformed into a pure version of her loving self. By the end of her dream, the cast-out parts of herself all merge into one—a pure, angelic reflection of herself—and just as Maikai is about to embrace this being in a big hug, she wakes up.

> It is a rainy morning outside the cave, but Maikai feels very different. She sits with the dragon and shares about her dream. The dragon asks her now to tell her where she feels that home is. Maikai says, "Here! And there," pointing to the town, "and there," pointing to the mountain, "and there," pointing in the direction of her homeland.
>
> The dragon tells her, "Now you know the feeling of home within—and as a result, you can find home anywhere. This will enable you to move into any situation or location and know home immediately. And wherever you do this, you teach home to others. There is an epidemic on this planet of people feeling homeless and lost, wandering. And the answer is always to welcome your Self—all of yourself—into yourSelf. For all you are is love."
>
> The End.

Silence.

As you both look out into the distance, the woman puts her shawl on her shoulders again. You sit together in the quiet, feeling the occasional breeze.

Then the woman speaks.

> My darling, thank you for your presence here tonight for Initiation Nine: Home. In any moment, you can take yourself home by embracing all the parts of you that you may not have yet wanted to. Is there a little feeling of tension? Here is an opportunity! Go into this feeling and invite it into your heart center. Welcome it. This is the energy. If you like, we can do this now together.

You nod, and she gently places her hand on your heart. And you feel so instantly loved, cared for, blessed, at peace, and grateful. You feel tears coming to your eyes at this sudden influx of love now, and you fully receive it by deepening your breath.

Instantly you see within yourself a space that must be the great hall of your own heart. Seven circles of light float in a perfect circle around you in the hall. You feel your heart go to each of these circles, connecting directly to them, creating a line of light directly to each glowing sphere, making you the center of a seven-pointed star. You feel upheld. You feel whole. You feel empowered. You feel gracious and grateful and full! It is a blissful feeling.

As you watch, these spheres begin to drift into other colors, other shapes, and then you witness them shifting into what you would deem negative feelings, emotions of fear, anger, and sadness, among others. Although the light remains strong between you and the feeling, you notice you are not as comfortable as before when these were perfect glowing spheres of love.

The woman speaks.

> *Now is the initiation. Even as you see these seven seemingly negative emotions floating around you, emotions you very much dislike, return yourself to the love feeling of origination, of love light. Imprint the memory of the spheres of light over these emotions to help you with your task. Breathe and receive. Use your vision. Notice what you see, what you feel, how these seven are acting. In every moment, the heart beam of connection is unwavering and strong. The energy exchange*

is felt for both. What does welcoming feel like? Welcome these energies home.

She begins to sing a rhythmic tribal song as you witness these energies, knowing your test is one of welcoming. It is uncomfortable to sit in the presence of these parts of yourself you have deemed "negative," "bad," or "horrible." You know that they started out as glowing spheres of love light, but in this moment, it is hard to remember. You encourage yourself to be present with them by looking directly at each of these seven energies.

I invite you into my heart, you say to them. And one by one, each walks into your heart's great receiving hall. Here you can see them more closely, although you don't necessarily feel peace and comfort.

Remembering Maikai, you say to them, *I welcome you here, and you can stay as long as you want. I know you are confused parts of me that want to give me the best life. I honor this about you. I even made you tea; please enjoy yourself while you are here.*

You find yourself looking even more closely at each energy, and you notice that at the center of each of these beings is a small glowing light. You didn't notice this before, but there it is. The center of each of these is the glowing light of love. You can see it! You feel compassion flooding into your body from all directions at this awareness.

At the center of each of these parts of you is the light of life essence, LOVE, that is the center of who You truly are. When you spot this, you feel your heart connecting with the light here in each of the seven shapes, instantly and easily.

You watch as they begin to change, sensing your love flowing to them. They flicker and morph, and before long, you witness these as seven balls of light floating around you once again. One of the spheres is directly in front of you, and it centers upon your heart. You see it coming gently towards you, slightly shrinking in size, until it reaches your heart center and morphs directly into your chest.

One by one, each of the seven spheres of light does this, until you are standing in the empty hall, feeling full and whole. You bask in this feeling of fullness, possibility, and strength within you now.

The woman's song comes to an end, and you feel quite different.

She says to you,

> *Home is where you welcome yourself. Home is within you now. You will find home wherever you go, and you will bring this vibration of home to all others you touch. Thank you for going through this initiation with me. I am honored, and I bow to the light that you are.*

You both stand up to look out at the view once more, and she gives you a hug before walking into the house. You meander through the hanging garden and walk back down the long, straight pathway to the center of the circle, where I am waiting for you.

Welcome home.

Namaste.

Ahom

Initiation Ten

Ahhhh, welcome!

Hold my hands and close your eyes.

Center your focus in the column of space between us.

See a golden staff as tall as your body, with a heart outlined in its center, about three-fourths of the way up the staff. The staff is pristine pure gold, straight, slender, and strong.

The heart shape in the middle lines up perfectly with your own heart.

Now forget the body for a moment and become this golden staff.

Trace the parts of you that you are as this staff.

Let the gold energy inform your cells—not as your body, but as this staff of gold.

Feel one with this.

And release this image.

Here we are, aiming at number TEN on our wheel—ten, our first double-digit number. And we walk forward, side by side; there is plenty of room here.

You look ahead, still feeling the tingle of the golden energy of the heart staff imprinted in your body's cells. At first, we see a vast emptiness. We keep walking.

> Down, down, down the path,
>
> Walking the path, down the path,
>
> Down, down, down, the path,
>
> Walking the midway path.

You begin to smell the scent of incense, subtle and very pleasing, filling your body with calm, a deepening of relaxation in the muscles. You begin to hear bustling sounds, other people, and you look up to see that the incense is coming from the small stand of a vendor. It seems he is selling little metal figurines of deities or holy figures. Looking around, you see before you a marketplace—dusty streets, a lot of pale brown in what appears to be a desert region. You feel enticed to stop at the stall with the religious figurines, and for a moment you lose yourself in the detail of the artist's designs.

You feel the inner pull to keep walking, so you do. This place feels very safe, even though there are many people here and many energies. You don't feel distracted by the vendors or the need to see what everyone is selling; you feel a pull to walk down this wide pedestrian street towards something. The further you walk, the stronger the pull to this place. What place? You'll know it when you see it, when you feel it.

After walking a little further, you see a stately building ahead of you. Getting closer, you realize it is a temple! It appears rectangular with another rectangular cap on top, with no points or peaks. It feels very exotic, while at the same time very comforting and familiar.

You look up as you continue to the entrance, and you notice arranged around the base of the roof are sculptures of the same deities being sold by the vendor. These are more robust, as they are much bigger, and you can feel the unique energies they radiate: welcoming, loving, guarding, guiding, and supporting. You reach the steps up to the entrance and approach the doorway.

When you walk inside, you are delighted by the amount of gold you see! Everywhere are statues, medallions, sculptures, and reliefs made of gold, painted with occasional bright red, blue, and green accents. This place feels rich with energy — energy that feels like wealth and happiness and laughter and joy. Abundance! That word seems to summarize the space beautifully.

Although there were many people outside, this space seems empty. You turn a few circles at the entryway, taking in all the beautiful golden art on the walls, columns, and ceiling. Directly in front of you, about ten feet from the entrance, is a large altar space. Within the rails that wrap around this altar is an expanse of stone floor, parts of it covered with a yellow mat, and beyond, up a few steps, is an area filled with golden art that depicts stories of this place's great avatars. You lose yourself in the intricacies of the detail in these sculptures and reliefs.

GONG!

You hear a gong sound that starts gently, but quickly increases in volume. Despite its gentle beginning, your heart is racing by the end of its swell. You feel your body give way to the vibrations, and yet you're not quite sure what to do. Simultaneously, you turn to see in the far corner of the room a man dressed in yellow who is holding a large mallet and striking the gong.

GONG!

Again it sounds as the first reverberations fade. This time you remind yourself it's just a gong and you can relax more. You take a deep breath as you listen and let the sound waves move through your body.

GONG!

It sounds a third time, and this time you feel prepared. Surely in this room of gold, a very pure vibration is being delivered throughout your body. You feel your muscles relaxing even more deeply as you place your attention on your body until the gong sound fades completely.

The man in yellow walks away, disappearing behind the large altar space. The room feels very clean after the sound passes, seeming extra silent.

Someone is coming out from behind the altar space directly in front of you, black-haired and wearing a long white robe. They bow to you. Only when they get closer do you realize it is a woman with her hair coiled up in two beautiful circles on the sides of her head.

> *Welcome to Initiation Ten: The Truth of the Wealth Within. I am the Guardian of the Glories of Gold. Look around you! You see gold everywhere. It is real gold. It carries a vibration of wealth, richness, fullness, freedom, prosperity, harmony, happiness, and fulfillment. This is the temple where you take this within, from without. Breathe this in now.*

She opens a gate in the railing between you and welcomes you into the altar space. You notice you are barefoot, as is she, and you step inside onto the yellow mat, which feels softer than the stone floor and much warmer. You feel it welcome the imprints and energy of your feet. You have never imagined that a mat could feel welcoming, but this is exactly how it feels.

The woman brings you straight in, leading you up three steps into a portion of the temple that was harder to see from outside the railing, being partially obscured by sculptures and statues of gold. As you pass these statues, you feel a noticeable tingling in your arms and legs, a very strong energy. The lighting shifts from natural light to what seems like electric light, and just a few steps in, you're surrounded in every direction by gold—beautiful life-size sculptures, reliefs, paintings, and statues.

In the center of this smaller gold-filled chamber is a chair, which looks like an ordinary wooden chair, but made of gold. The woman invites you to sit in this chair, which you find much more comfortable than it looks. Immediately as you sit, you feel a sensation rising from the base of your spine, flowing swiftly through your body in an upward direction. Your arms rest on the arms of the chair, and you feel this energy flowing down your arms and out your hands very noticeably. It is a good feeling, and you feel calm, paired with a sensation of swiftness that takes you a few breaths to get used to.

The woman speaks.

> *Welcome to the inner chamber of total abundance. Here we guide you through a process to know your own wealth and prosperity as sensations throughout your body, so you can come to know these easily in the life you are creating for yourself as a human being in this incarnation. Here is where you can receive the imprint—and we would say the depth of understanding—of what you are capable of.*
>
> *Feel into this space here, the chair and the air around you, but also the masks and sculptures, the statues and works of art that are all pure gold. I will guide you inside the gold now.*

She directs you to relax your head onto the high back of the chair, then lightly touches your temples. Your vision shifts to face a large golden lion head above you on the wall. You are small in comparison to this large gold sculpture. Your vision expands, and you see yourself shrinking down small enough to go into this lion head through the cheek, to stand inside the gold, fully surrounded by it, as if you are merging with the gold, becoming part of it.

The woman instructs you,

> *Breathe deeply here.*
>
> *Notice in your body the scent, the taste, and the feeling in your skin of merging with gold.*
>
> *If you have any resistance, remember this simplicity: gold is purely an element of the earth, as is quartz crystal, a native substance of this beautiful planet.*
>
> *As you are merged inside this gold, what flavor is the energy here?*

Tuning into this, you notice the energy is bright, golden, soft, energizing, strong, comforting, activating, invigorating… Like vitality. Like innovation. Like security. Like flow. Like ease. Like smiles.

The woman hears you telepathically and continues speaking.

> *Yes, the life force of the element gold is very strong, and it serves a great purpose in assisting us to know our own life force—knowing what we are capable of, as in being, not only doing. Here inside this sculpture, we are being, and yet amplified, merged with the energy of gold we feel so strongly in the body. Feel it pulsing out, vibrating out from within. Do you feel this—as one?*

She lightly lifts her hands from your head, and you are instantly back in the chair.

> *You must know for yourself, from within yourself, your wealth, your value, your (you're) gold. You must be alert to the vital force within you. You must be aware that your beingness is it already, in addition to your doing.*

Stand up now and follow me. I will lead you in movements of the gold within. I will watch and make adjustments if any are needed for the greatest energy flow. Know that the gold around you now is helping you, supporting you, amplifying the experience to assist in imprinting this feeling into the body.

You stand up, and she moves the chair to the far wall.

You go through the following mudras as instructed, and she is with you. As you do so, you feel the energy imprinting into your muscle memory and into your cells, deepening this knowingness in your body.

She begins.

Wealth Within.

First, make a triangle with your hands—a golden pyramid. Hold this at your heart level.

Center yourself in your heart energy, pressing the pyramid against your heart center.

Center yourself in Knowing of Being as you raise the pyramid to your forehead.

Center yourself in Knowing of Cosmic Eternal Connection as you raise the pyramid to press it to the top of your head, with your crown chakra shining right through the center of it.

Bringing the hands down into prayer position, open the palms outward, making the pyramid shape again, pressing it outward, centering yourself in Knowing of Connection to All of Humanity.

Bringing the hands to prayer position again, point the fingers downward and open the palms towards the body in an upside-down pyramid that you press against your sacral chakra, centering yourself in Knowing of the Power of Your Creation

Sliding the hands down and outward, still making a pyramid, bend forward at the waist and knees to press this pyramid into the earth, centering yourself in Knowing of Earth Connection and Reverence.

Slowly coming back up, let your hands naturally fold in prayer at the heart, closing the eyes, centering yourself in Knowing of Self, that you are a spark of the Divine All, and for this existence, you give thanks.

The woman continues.

> *Why wealth within? As we go out into creation, contributing our own creation as creator gods and goddesses, the wealth within becomes the compass, the map for aiming ourselves in the direction of total wealth. Not wealth in one aspect only—say, golden coins, or family—but wealth in all directions, as guided by your soul's unique pathway of experience and growth—your full sphere of wealth, for the balanced life is the golden life.*
>
> *I honor you for your presence here today. I honor your body for receiving this imprinting. I honor your mind for remembering the mudra movements and incorporating them into your life as a playful practice. Centering in this present moment, we close our eyes.*

She begins to sing, a most unusual honoring song in a language you do not recognize, and you feel inside a desire to dance, to laugh, to shine, to do somersaults! It is an interesting feeling, as you are standing still, but you watch it and allow it to be, letting the smile grow on your face as she continues her beautiful song blessing.

When she stops singing, you open your eyes, and it is finished. You are in the space at the center of the circle of initiations. You turn around, and I am here.

Blessings, golden one. You are initiated.

All my love and gratitude to you for playing with us in this way.

Ahom

Initiation Eleven

I am here. It is a pleasure to be with you here now, in this space of no time.

Breathe with me as we stand in the center of the circle.

Inhaling - - - pause - - - Exhaling - - - pause - - -

Inhaling - - - pause - - - Exhaling - - - pause - - -

Inhaling - - - pause - - - Exhaling - - - pause - - -

Now we begin our walk to Initiation Eleven!

Looking up towards number ELEVEN in our circle, you see two points in the distance. As you walk closer, you see two towers, cylindrical, reminding you of two grain silos. The land around us is flat, and these are the only things you see in the area ahead of you. Now closer, it is clear that silos are what they are.

As the empty space turns to trodden grass, you see a worn pathway in front of you, a mixture of grass and sandy soil. You walk easily towards the two towers. Now you can make out something up high, connecting the towers to each other. It appears to be a bridge.

Your body feels light, your feet easy on the earth, and your heart feels relaxed. You wonder delightedly what is ahead of you. Remembering that this is Initiation Eleven, you laugh to yourself; these two buildings actually look like they make the number 11!

As you approach, you see that the buildings are made of large, light gray bricks in very smooth masonry, making them perfectly circular. There appears to be far more attention to detail than you would see in a basic grain silo. This excites you a little, and you continue walking.

The path seems to lead to the lefthand tower, and you pause for a moment to feel in your body which way to go. Yes, left is perfect now. You move towards the small door on the front of the left tower. Against its vast size, the door looks miniscule, but as you approach, you can see it is a full-sized door.

As you get close, you feel the gravity of this tall building. You're within its inner energy field now, and your own energy field is already interacting with that of the building. You notice this easily in your body and feel a real connection. It feels loving. How fascinating—you have perhaps never noticed before that a building, especially a simplistic seemingly industrial building like this one, could put off a loving vibration in this way.

It feels so good that you take your time in opening the door. It squeaks when you finally open it, making a very loud echo throughout the whole interior.

Hello!

You call out, listening to the beautiful echo of your voice in the tall room. You are surprised to see that the tower is completely hollow inside. There is nothing here but two large windows at the top, with quite a bit of sunlight streaming in. It isn't too dark, but it is definitely dimmer than outside. As your eyes adjust, you play in the echo.

Ah-oooo!

Your sound lingers in the space for several seconds. You playfully throw out syllables and sounds as you marvel at what your ears and body are experiencing from the vibrations you share. You twirl in the center of this structure, watching the ceiling as you do. You close your eyes to shake off the dizziness, and when you open them, you see a man standing by the door. He is emanating a soft golden light, and you are not frightened in any way. You feel even more calm, and you wonder who he is. He has a beard, not too long, and graying golden-brown hair sticking out from under his floppy farmer's hat—or is it more of a wizard's hat? You feel an inner smile at this thought.

He speaks.

> *Welcome. I am the keeper of these storehouses, and I greet you with confidence and an open heart. Welcome to Initiation Eleven: Balance. I thank you for coming, and now with your permission, I will close the door and begin.*

You nod to him, and he closes the door. Behind it is a lever that you hadn't seen. He walks over to it and pulls it towards himself, using his whole body to maneuver it. You hear an unusual noise — then the walls begin to move! They are turning counterclockwise, and all up and down them, wooden boards begin to extend outward from the wall. You can see them spiraling upwards around the cylinder.

When the wooden boards lock into place, you marvel to see they form a floating staircase, with one side of the stairs held by the walls of the storehouse and the other side hovering in midair. There is space beneath and between each stair, and no handrail on the left side. You get the impression that climbing this staircase may be wild, or even dangerous! One slip, and your foot could go right through the stairs... Simultaneously, you are absolutely delighted that someone designed a building with round walls and a staircase that appears and disappears.

The man speaks.

> *The ascending spiral. We will go together, ascending counterclockwise. Please walk with me.*

He gives no other instruction, so you walk over to the first step and stand side by side with him.

INITIATION ELEVEN

Ascending the summit. Before we begin, I sense some apprehension in your heart field about the height, width, and distance of these stairs. Become aware of this, and let it float forward into your body's exterior energy field as a golden sphere of light. You don't have to let go of the apprehension; just look at it in front of your heart rather than inside it...

Beautiful! Now that you see it, can you hold it in your hands? Move it to the left and right. Allow it to fully detach from your inner body. Yes, do you feel this?

Now let us take one step up while holding this. You stand on the inside between me and the wall, and I will walk on the outside here.

You step up onto the first step together. It is wider and flatter than you imagined, with not so great a distance between the steps. It feels much gentler than you imagined climbing a staircase could be.

The man speaks.

I would like for you to carry this apprehension up the staircase with me. Let us take another step while holding this.

You step up another step, and this is easy too. Although you feel like it would be nice to hold onto something, your hands are engaged in holding the light sphere of your apprehension. You find it interesting that going up a single step could take so much attention.

> Yes, this is good. Step up again. Do you feel the balance and ease here? Find the focus of your attention while you continue holding the apprehension out in front of you—lovingly, of course—and moving up the stairs.

You begin slowly, maintaining a steady rhythm, at first pausing for a second or two on each step before going higher. You feel balanced and strong, and you find it no problem to hold the apprehension sphere as you go. The stepping becomes slightly more rhythmic as you step up one, then another with barely a pause, but still following the wise man's very slow and easy pace.

The man speaks.

> I am the Angel of the Ascent of the Summit.

Of course he is, you think to yourself, as you remember he did have an unearthly glow to him when you first saw him by the door.

The angel continues.

> In everyday Earth life, we encounter one summit after the next that we are to ascend, to climb. Summits come in all sizes and magnitudes, and at all levels of challenge. Here we create the experience of ascending to the summit, with the common feelings of apprehension, self-doubt, and perhaps fear—even questioning the point of it.
>
> Yet somewhere inside calls you. You have seen the high window above. You have seen the bridge outside before you entered. You know there is more, there is something greater at the summit, but you do not know if you can get there or how, or why you should try at all.

> *Step.*
>
> *Step.*
>
> *Step.*
>
> *Do these feelings seem familiar? Yet you have ascended the summit many times over and over again in just this lifetime alone—successfully! What is it that allows you to do this? Your Creatorship! Your vision! Your inner knowing. Your inner yearning, or burning, or passion, or pure desire. The sense of I WILL. And you do! Hoo-hoo!*

He practically jumps to celebrate his joy at the successes he speaks of, then looks at your hands.

> *Have you noticed the size of your sphere of apprehension since we began ascending? It is shrinking according to the size of your pure desire to reach the summit, to go through this initiation fully, to have the vision that will be opened to you from a view so high. Yes? Can you relax your arms and let the apprehension lift off on its own?*

You notice you are feeling much more comfortable, as you have already made it up many stairs, and you are feeling strong in your body—light, energetic, and easy. You drop your hands to your sides, and with your inner vision, you see the golden sphere lifting up and floating towards the light high at the top. It feels so good to let it go, to relax your arms, and you feel the feeling of freedom rushing into your limbs.

> *Ahhh yes, beautiful! I watched it go up and out the window up there; how beautiful to send this off to its perfect vibration, as your vibration is now lifting and lifting to an even higher place. Can you feel it?*

In fact, you can! You sense into your body and recognize an overall lightness that seems to be growing. You feel into the wall beside you and notice that there is an indentation, like an inverted handrail, which would help stabilize you if you needed it. You cannot easily see down to the floor due to the angle of the stairs, so you feel a sense of ease and confidence as you go up. You notice the energy of the angel is exactly the energy that most helps you feel strong and capable.

The angel speaks.

> *"Capability" is a subjective term, for what is the point of measurement: the task achieved, or the wisdom gained? Every human being is capable. And whatever each is aiming towards, the unique gifts and experiences that are lined up by the higher self are relative to the task at hand.*
>
> *There is never a question of whether one is capable—never! There is only a question of how the capability will be made manifest. And sometimes a person can have a different desire than their capability will guide them toward. Do you follow?*

You nod, feeling like you recognize the truth in this. Every human being is capable, yet what they achieve through their capabilities may not be what they set out to achieve. This may make them question whether they are truly capable, but because they did achieve something, they are capable; they can shift their awareness to see where their higher self set them up to go, which may be different from where they thought they were going...

Exactly right.

You are startled; you had not opened your mouth.

Yes, of course you are communicating telepathically with me. In fact, you may observe that I am not speaking to you either; you are hearing me in your inner ears.

As he says this, you turn to see that his mouth is closed like yours. And yet his voice seems to echo through the space, as if he is speaking aloud.

Effect! I add the echo in there for the effect. Hee hee! So, feeling into your capability now, notice we are halfway to the top. Let us pause at the next step to take in the new perspective.

You turn around as you come to the next step, and wow, it is a different world up here! You are now on the opposite side from the door, looking at the spiraling staircase cascading down the round walls behind you.

Feel the effort exerted to this point, and feel good, he says. *Welcome the self-congratulations! Welcome the "wow" feeling! It is good! We are here! Let us go on!*

Ascending is masculine in its energy, compared to descending, which is feminine. We must go against gravity here, ever upward, using our muscles, mental encouragement, effort, yes—but in a relaxed sense in our case. To reach the summit takes direction and effort! Yang energy, action energy! And here we are, doing it! Doesn't it feel good?

If we were to continue in this way indefinitely, there would come a point where it would become tiresome. You would experience some confusion, asking yourself, "Why isn't the good feeling here like the last time I ascended the summit?"

Well, because you would have taken out the summit experience by continuing with climbing to the next step, and the next, and the next—an eternal spiral staircase upward, and no way to get off of it! At least, no way you can see, because you keep stepping over the summit point and moving on to the next summit point.

The point is the point of it all! Feel the power of the ascent as we take these next steps. Absorb the beauty of this power.

Step.

Step.

Step.

You climb in silence now. You feel your body receiving this power. It feels invigorating; you have lost all hint of fear, and you are getting close to the ceiling! You feel your muscles in your arms, your spine straight and solid, fully supporting you in the easiest and lightest way. You feel excitement in your solar plexus, spreading out like sunlight to all parts of your body. You feel a smile in your heart center, and a very light vibration emanating off the top of your head. You feel empowered in the total sense of the word—and it feels amazing!

And here we are!

INITIATION ELEVEN

You take the final three steps together as the staircase spirals you up to a small landing at the very top of the building. You find an arched doorway through the gray bricks. On the other side is the bridge you saw from the ground, a sturdy-looking rope bridge. The angle of the boards tells you that the beautiful walkway has very little give. The ropes are thick, higher than your waist, and a thinner rope connects them to the boards in a spiderweb of netting, holding you very safely if you were to go across.

The angel speaks.

> *Perspective! You ascended the summit for the great bounty of a new perspective! And is it worth it? The soul ascends the spiral ladder of creation on its way back to Source by attaining one new perspective after another, thereby expanding perspective until the truth of total all-ness, total oneness, is known, is lived!*
>
> *That is one way to see it, anyway. Please allow your own wisdom to guide you through your ascent of summits in the way that you are led, inspired, and delighted to experience.*
>
> *So, here we are at the summit. Now, how do you take it in? How do you celebrate?*
>
> *It is very grand indeed, and as we know, you are capable, for here you are! What you set out to do at the beginning, you have achieved; you are here.*
>
> *Now. The secret to taking it in, to celebrating this?*
>
> *Bask.*
>
> *Yes, bask!*

> *Let us go out to see more, for this doorway blocks a lot of the view that is part of the delight and bounty of this perspective.*

You both walk out onto the bridge, and you enjoy how solid and safe it feels. But it is very high up! You are telling yourself you can do this, that you are capable. You are.

You ARE.

The beauty all around is surprising and delighting you so much that you release questioning your safety to receive this unparalleled view. Far below are rolling green hills in every direction, a true grassland, dark greens merging into light greens and busy greens meeting coarse greens. Birds are easy to spot from up here, although none seem to reside in these towers. You must be more than ten stories high, and yet you feel relaxed and capable even now.

The angel speaks.

> *Deep breath! That is one way to bask!*
>
> *Inhale the beauty of this moment, the beauty of your achievement—the beauty of you! The beauty of LIFE! The beauty of the feeling of ascension, and the feeling of arriving at the summit point.*

You take your time walking all the way across the bridge, and finally, in perfect timing, when you have had just enough of this beautiful view, you enter the arched doorway of the other tower.

> *And here we are. I leave you with the Angel of the Descent.*

INITIATION ELEVEN

A beautiful woman greets you, wearing a simple dress and outdoor leather boots. She smiles and bows to you.

Welcome, and congratulations on your Ascent of the Summit. I honor you here. And now, together, we Descend the Spiral of Creation.

The stairs are already extended in this tower, looking exactly the same as in the first tower. You feel this part will be easy. If you can go up, you can surely go down!

The angel speaks.

The descent is often a part skipped over, for there have come to be judgments of many kinds about the descent. However, it is just as important as the ascent. The glory, the focus, the excitement seems to build up to the summit, and at the achievement point, there is often a hesitation, for the descent is seen as perhaps not as fun or productive or important. Knowing these are all simply projections of judgment, you can become a master of the descent, finding the same enjoyment and expansion of self through coming down.

> Step.
>
> Step.
>
> Step.

Your pace is perfectly slow, but even and easy. You are very high up, but as before, you are safely between the Angel and the wall as you descend clockwise.

The angel speaks.

> Many people want to rush the descent, if they even face it at all. Of course, you cannot climb to the peak of a mountain without coming back down, yet the minds of peak achievers are often trained on the next summit to ascend, and thus not present for the many gifts of the descent. Be present now with our descent; feel it in your body. Notice what you feel.

You first notice that you feel relaxed, calm, and easy. You feel whole. You feel supported.

> Yes. Here, gravity is a great support for the direction you are moving in, as well as the surface beneath your feet, your own body, and the elements around you. You may notice that your heart is more relaxed than it was during the ascent.

> And let's look deeper here. Descent is the time for unraveling. All the energy that spiraled into the ascent of the summit, now in its unraveling will be perfectly ready for the next ascent—but only if we balance the coils in this opposite directional spiral. Can you see?

It is amazing to look up at the height you came from and down to the depth you are moving toward as you spiral downward in a clockwise direction. It seems to be going much faster than it did in the other tower. Is this due to the aid of gravity, or the sense of ease in your relaxed body?

The angel speaks.

> I invite you to take all the gifts from the descending now, as these final stairs round us down. Relax and receive. Release and let the unwinding happen. Allow it to feel like an internal massage. Allow this space for yourself. Allow the descent to be, to exist for all, and to be recognized in all its glory and importance.

You come to the three final steps.

Three, two, one ... and you're on the ground again.

You pause with the angel as you feel the stillness and the weight of the energy, which is slightly different as you come down to the ground. You feel an immediate connection to Mother Earth through your feet. You feel an awareness of your body, more physical than before, especially compared to how it felt at the top of the summit. You feel fully present, relaxed, and full, eager to rest. Not from tiredness, but more from the joy of celebrating this ease, this feeling of deserving, and this sense of completion.

The angel speaks.

> *Grounded. The power of being grounded. The potential of being in the grounded state. Reconnected to Earth. Reconnected to pure potential, pure freedom. Here, you are ready to create again, unwound from the Before, and ready to go with your full energy into the Becoming.*
>
> *Welcome this! And celebrate your patience and your own immersion in the most balanced and nourishing thing you could ever do for yourself after ascending a summit: unwinding and grounding.*
>
> *Bless you for receiving this Initiation Eleven: Balance. Bring this into your heart as a dozen love-filled roses bursting with color, fragrance, and life!*

In your inner vision, you can see her produce a dozen red roses bursting with life, and she places them inside your heart, where their blooms fill you with radiance. You feel their glorious energy shining out from your heart, moving through your blood and all over your entire body, this feeling of accomplishment and deep peace. Your body knows more perhaps than your mind does at this moment. And you find yourself bowing to her, thanking her as she walks you to the door.

You step back out into the sunshine and find yourself instantly in the center with me.

I welcome you back.

I feel the beauty all throughout you!

And I bless your rose-filled heart!

Ahom

INITIATION TWELVE

Now come with me into the center circle of our circle of Twelve Initiations.

Let us take a glance in all the directions, starting at
ONE...

TWO...

THREE...

FOUR...

FIVE...

SIX...

SEVEN...

EIGHT...

NINE...

TEN...

ELEVEN...

Pausing here...

What a full and beautiful space we have created!

Close your eyes for a moment and feel all the colors and flavors of each of these journeys, each of the gifts received, each of the offerings made.

Let the energy of all eleven of these dance around you.

Feel the fullness of this beautiful wheel of initiations.

And now, let us turn to face the number TWELVE, the top of the wheel, our true north. And we walk straight there together now into this Initiation Twelve. I will be behind you, as always. I honor each of the footsteps you take now into this final initiation.

As you walk, you feel a marked balance, as if you had handrails to either side of you, perfectly distanced, such that if you were to grab one rail in each hand, you could easily lift yourself up off your feet. You imagine doing this now.

Your hands fill with the rails, and now you are on a bridge. It is the most beautiful bridge you have ever seen, with green mosses growing from the sides and dripping over the edges, dotted with colorful flowers, some small and delicate, some vibrant and hearty. The bridge is very sturdy and does not shake, although it is just the perfect size for one person to walk.

You can see quite a distance around you on this bridge—a beautiful mountainous landscape, so lovely that you find yourself enjoying each step as you cross this scenic chasm. You look over the side and see below you a distant valley with a tiny river at the bottom. You imagine the river is not so tiny, but the distance makes you perceive it this way. The landscape is green in every direction, with sloping hills before and behind you. It is vast and magnificent, and you feel very safe and easy here. You also notice you feel very balanced, even lifted up, as if you are very physically supported by this bridge and by the energy that is holding it up. It is a comfort to notice and feel this, and you relax even more into enjoying the walk across this beautiful mountain bridge.

As you approach the other side, you begin to see more details. A mountain reveals itself before you, and it too is covered in flowers in waves of different colors. What a beautiful scene! You feel it drawing you toward it like a living being, as if it is magnetizing you to itself. Your feet happily continue walking across.

The bridge soon connects to a gently sloping grassy area, and you step off the bridge onto the rich living earth. There is a feeling of LIFE everywhere here! You are breathing in the vitality, the life essence, floating in the very air around you. You can easily feel the life in the sweet breeze rustling a distant tree and the tall grasses growing nearby.

The hill slopes dramatically upward in front of you, covered in grass, and you feel compelled to press your hands into it, so you walk forward a few steps and fall into the earth, palms out, offering your own vitality to the ground as a gift of your gratitude and honor to be in this sacred, vital place.

As you do this, you notice that you are also receiving a very good feeling through your palms—a feeling of invigoration, gentle but sweeping, like a bath of perfect temperature that sweeps over the body in warmth. You bask in this for a few moments.

You see the path curves around to the right, and you begin to head in that direction. It is slightly worn, just enough to be noticeable. It wanders through the low grasses, and follows the curve of the mountain, turning left out of your field of vision. You begin walking. Your heart and eyes are filled with so much love and reverence for this mind-expanding BEAUTY that surrounds you now!

To your right is a downward slope, and across the valley, you see another gorgeous mountain dotted with flowers against shades of green. The depth only adds to the beauty. The sky is bright blue, with occasional swiftly moving thin white clouds flowing by. To your left is the mountain you just gifted your energy to, and which gifted you hers.

You arrive at the curve in the path that you could not see beyond, and now you see a few small trees as the path leads you into a gentle wood. These trees seem more like ancient shrubs that have grown to enormous sizes, with thin, knobby trunks and branches creating a network of connection in every direction. You can see through the treetops easily to the blue sky beyond, as they do not yet have their full crown of leaves, but are budding now. It feels delightful to continue into this beautiful space, even though you wonder where exactly you are going. You feel full of energy and vitality, and you take another deep breath of this beautiful and pure living air!

Entering the small wood, you feel a shift in the energy. It's noticeably more intimate, a closer feeling. You are admiring the way all the branches cross, taking in the shapes between them, when you hear a sound.

You look ahead, and standing in the wood is a small woman. She appears very old, yet full of life force, and she has a warm smile on her face. You feel her smile coming very strongly from her heart, and you are moved by the genuineness of this full heart smile.

> *Welcome! We are so grateful you have come, and we honor you and welcome you to the Living Forest of Vitality, and to Initiation Twelve: Rebirth. I am the Lady of the Wood, and I will be your guide through the forest and then on to the Waterfall of Rebirth. Shall we?*

You feel waves of gratitude and excitement wash over you as you hear her words.

She continues.

> *You feel the essence of life here in this place, yes? You are welcome to it. You are welcome to take it in, and allow yourself to thrive as you do so. For the more you thrive in yourself, the more we thrive in ourselves; such is the nature of the woods here, and the mountains, and all that is living here. The more*

> *you are thriving in your own way, the more you give out energy to the organism that is planet Earth. And the more she soaks in this vibration, this vitality, the more she thrives.*
>
> *If you make this your mission, to thrive every day, you cannot be doing anything but fulfilling your greatest purpose on Earth. You may feel you are not "doing" something, you know, but the truth is, yes, of course, you ARE doing it! You are doing perhaps the most important thing you can do, which is contributing your vitality, your vibrant life energy to the life of this microcosm, and thus this macrocosm. You see?! Hee hee hee!*

You wind through the woods, wondering if this woman isn't one of these trees come to life; she moves like you might imagine a tree would walk. She is full of life and energy as she is leading you. You notice the new buds beginning to come forth on these trees, filling you with an even deeper level of life force, life essence, and vitality as you feel their bursting vibrance radiating energy and power outward from their tips.

The woman speaks.

> *And what is rebirth? It is a word often used, you know; "I need a rebirth," you may say. "I am going through a total rebirth." But can you rebirth yourself? Can you get back into the womb space and truly re-birth yourself?*
>
> *Of COURSE you can! Although it takes great presence of mind to experience this fully, and a great deal of trust—in yourself, in your safety, in your original divine spark.*

INITIATION TWELVE

> *YES! Did you not think of this? Yes, it is true! Trust in your divine spark is most important in the rebirthing process. We will experience the rebirth in the Waterfall of Rebirth, which is not too far down the path once we exit the wood.*

You look ahead and see the trees thinning, and you realize you are almost out of this magical intimate forest.

The woman continues.

> *The gift of the wood is the intimacy it offers you. See that your energy field has come in closer now, and you can really feel yourself. Before we exit these magical trees, scan your space—your personal energetic space, which extends off the physical body quite a bit—and see if any energies come into view that may need a little attention. How do you spot these? You sense with your feeling sense or your inner vision any place that feels sticky, thicker, darker, or hardened. That's all; it's simple. Feel into your field now. You will find the trees are most helpful with this.*

She pauses as you stand in the pathway, and you close your eyes. You reach out to the tree next to you and wrap your hand around a small, sturdy branch. As you feel its energy, you immediately see your energy field more vividly. It is easy to scan the glowing cocoon around yourself, as well as your physical body field. You can see where there is sticky energy, and you allow your attention to be there, as the woman said.

> *Beautifully done! Here, noticing the stickier energy, invite the vital life force of this forest directly into it, using your breath. In every inch, there are a billion trillion particles of vital force in the air here in this forest. Breathe them into your body now,*

> making a special effort to siphon some breaths directly into the places that you feel to be thicker, stickier. You need not assign any meaning to these energies you detect, but offer them loving attention, and gift them the vitality of the air in this wood.

You watch these energies with your inner vision as you breathe vital life force into them from the fresh mountain air combined with the bursting new life from these special trees. You feel a very gentle opening in your spaces of thicker energy that feels good, full, and easy.

> Beautifully done! You may open your eyes whenever you feel complete. Let us move through the curtain of the parting trees as we descend to the Waterfall of Rebirth.

You walk out through the trees and are greeted by a fresh gust of breeze that is refreshingly clean, and slightly different energetically than the breeze in the wood—more like a lifting, an energy that would easily carry a bird in flight. This energy feels good. Then you see a very gently descending staircase, turning and winding down the side of this lovely mountain. It is shaded by larger trees with dark needles. The air feels more moist here as you begin to walk down the stairs.

The woman speaks.

> Going down, down into the womb space, making the agreement to come to Earth—it is never done unjoyfully. The soul never makes the choice without the passion or desire to be here! This may be hard to remember when the physical, tangible aspects of being incarnate cause pain to the body and

emotional vehicle. Knowing that we are born eternal helps to give perspective on the difficulties at times. Yet the physical can seem so very separate, so very alone. We know, we know...

Yet you chose this! Joyfully know that you did not take on anything you are not capable of! Haven't you learned about "capability"? Hee hee! So, as we descend, joyfully delight in this beautiful journey from the vastness of the mountain above to the smallness and darkness of the womb space below. And here we go...

The stairs descend, gently turning with the rocks as they define a passageway down of varying steepness. But the descent is easy, and you feel clear, solid in yourself. You notice a new energy in your body, fresh, and you realize it's the feeling of confidence, steadily expanding within you. You are capable. You did choose this. You would not choose something you are not capable of surviving—no, thriving in!

The woman speaks.

Yes, indeed! The many things that seem like hardships all along the way—perhaps YOU, your wise higher self, put them there for you to grow in the most perfect way? What if these seeming hardships were really great gifts to yourself, from yourself—gifts that have allowed you to know deeper parts of YOU, to stretch and expand in bigger ways than you could have ever done without them?

You feel the vibration of her words landing somewhere deep in your energy field as the path takes a noticeable turn to the right, then to the right again. It's like a natural spiral staircase, although wider. You notice the sound of rushing water becoming more and more present in your field of listening. Now it is becoming so loud that you know water must be very nearby.

The woman speaks.

> *Do you hear this? That frequency, that rushing water sound—that is a clearing in itself. Add a little intention to it, and whoosh, you are cleared! Shall we now?*

You wholeheartedly agree, which the woman feels. She pauses to stand on a small rock to the side of the natural staircase and speaks in a clear, loud voice.

> *I declare the intention for the total rebirth of you, beautiful human being, now!*

> *I declare a cleanse from the bottom up for you, a clearing from the inside out, and a washing out of perspective, so the new, true, pure perspective will be in the forefront now, a broader awareness, a higher consciousness.*

> *May this water cleanse be a total rebirth of yourself into greater perception of the Truth of your existence! The choices you have made for yourself before birth and in life—all were always perfect, and you will have the clarity to know that they will continue to be so.*

> *The total rebirth of sense of self aligned with the highest truth that You Are.*

> *Like the great I AM, You ARE. And now you move into the conscious creator God-self, as you were created to be. Made*

INITIATION TWELVE

> *in the image of the Great Creator, may you now be reborn to perfectly perceive this image: the Creator God that you truly are!*

You feel waves of energy, like wind rippling upwards through your body, as she speaks these words. And after another deep breath, you descend the final few stairs. They are still turning slightly, and as you round the last turn, you behold the sight of an immense waterfall before you. It falls into a beautiful circular pool, and there are rainbows everywhere from the gleaming sunlight bouncing off the water particles that dance in midair between you and the falling water. You wonder for a moment how close you will actually get to this waterfall.

The wise woman guides you around the right side of the pool, stepping carefully on the stones, and you both enter a corridor of rock that leads behind the waterfall. As you walk through the opening, it is considerably darker than outside, and at first you can hardly see anything at all. The thunderous sound of the water is now so intense, you would have to yell to be heard above it. Before you can figure out how to ask the woman what is next, you hear her voice in your head, as clearly as if you were talking together in a quiet parlor.

> *Blackness of the womb. Pause here and remember for a moment. Remember with me the moment you chose to come to Earth for this life, the moment you chose your parents, the between-life space, the darkness of nothing. Yet from the blackness comes the birth of creation, the birth of life, the expression of the all as a unique individual spark: YOU.*

As she speaks the word "YOU," she lightly touches your third eye. Immediately your vision shifts to the space between lives. It looks like outer space here, all blackness and distant stars. A great neutrality takes over your body as you surrender to this feeling of clarity and simplicity.

You see your parents on Earth, and your wise self has a sense of all that is to come, all that was before, and the knowing of what lies before you to enhance and expand the experience of your soul. You feel an inner elation at the depth of wisdom and expansion your soul will gain from choosing a life through these two human beings. And you say, "Yes!"

You see a point of light in front of you, and you lock onto this point. This is the seed point of the egg and sperm meeting, and you allow yourself to be magnetically drawn to this spark of light. As you get closer, it gets bigger and bigger, becoming a star, and its magnetism is blissfully powerful as you surrender yourself to it fully, allowing yourself to be taken by this beautiful star, surrounded by it, and immersed in it, until once inside its center, you are again in blackness.

You feel the wise woman lightly touch your forehead again, and you are immediately back in the corridor, her voice still easily audible in your head.

> *The blackness of the womb. Total nourishment, sustenance, and growth here, safety and support. Breathe into the comfort of this place of the mystery of life. From the womb, we rebirth ourselves into the knowing of all that we are.*

As you are taking a few slow steps together, the hallway curves slightly to the left. Following this, you find yourself only a few steps away from standing directly behind the waterfall.

Here You Are. It is time for the rebirth.

You stand facing the pouring water and listen to her instructions.

She speaks with great enthusiasm.

> *Now is everything! Now is all we have! Now is the moment of your REBIRTH!*
>
> *Now bring your awareness to the bottoms of your feet, directly connected to the Earth. Let anything old, tense, dense, or dull flow downward out through the bottoms of your feet into the rock to be received by Mother Earth and reused as fodder for new growth.*

You feel energy sliding easily down your body and through your legs, being gratefully received by the Earth. As you relax your mind into focusing more on this feeling, it feels good, and you let it flow.

> *Now bring your awareness to the waterfall before you, and prepare yourself to walk through to the other side. You can trust that there is flat rock that will support you, even when the weight of the falling water seems to be a lot. When you are ready, clear your mind, and begin the walk through.*

The last bits of any tension are flowing down your legs and out through your feet into the Earth. You feel light and unusually clear. You walk forward, noticing each step. As the water begins to wet you from the proximity, you hear again the woman's voice in your head.

> *Breathe. Let the breath be the central point of focus. Return here in every moment. Stay here. Breathe ... and Let Go.*

Breathing deeply, you step under the falling water.

Everything becomes white light. Instantaneously you are transported to a space that feels like nothingness, whiteness, all light. It is silent, eternal here, not positive or negative; it simply is. For this timeless moment, you feel completely and beautifully detached from everything, while at the same time, you feel crystal clear, wide open. Empty. Alive. At One. One with all. Eternal Peace. Eternal Light. You Are.

You hear the woman's voice.

> *The space of return. The bliss of Divine union. Here you are. No body. No time. Simply All. Allness. Oneness. Bliss. The bliss of awareness of being. You are this. You are this Allness. You are this vast. You are this Light. You are this Love. You are. You Are ...You ARE!*

As the white light starts to fade, you begin to make out the water falling as you remember to breathe and keep your feet moving forward. You wonder how much time has passed in the oneness of the white light, and yet your awareness now goes to your body. The water beats down upon you more strongly now, and you raise your hands up, offering your own upward energy to this vital force that rains down upon you. REBIRTH!

You then feel drawn to fold forward in surrender to the downward force of the water's drops, letting it pound upon your back. The sound is surreal; rushing water is all you hear. And you receive the deeply cleansing vibration of these thunderous sound waves penetrating every cell of your body.

After a moment, you feel complete, ready to walk to the other side. The falling water lessens in intensity, and soon you stand in an inch of water upon a smooth rock platform that runs like an underwater bridge clear to the other side of the pool.

As you step beyond the water drops completely, you turn around to take in the waterfall with your eyes, and you feel compelled to drop to your knees. You fold forward in a humble pose like a child, honoring the great power and majesty in this water. You notice your mind is completely clear. Your pathway is easy to see before you, and you give gushing gratitude to the rock below you. You feel the Earth joyously receive this as you notice a wave of warmth swirling through the water around your body.

When you feel complete with your gratitude, you stand up, born again, still vibrating from the roaring sound waves and physical force of the water falling into you. Turning around, you walk across the pool, where you see your guide appear on the other side.

Yes, you have made it! Rebirth has occurred!

Welcome the curiosity, the not knowing, the new eyes that you have now to see things differently than ever before. Welcome seeing the world with the innocence of a child. Welcome the phrase in any moment, "I do not know what anything is for." Welcome the phrase, "I do not know what my brother or sister truly needs." Welcome the phrase, "I need do nothing."

See how these float you into a new life, a new reality—one where you demonstrate your Creator God power, as you manifest through your own vibration exactly what you most desire.

This is the new you. This is the True You. Go forth in fullness of the light that you truly are, and bless all things simply by Being. You are! You Are! You ARE! And so it is!

She bows to you and offers you a white sheet to wrap around yourself to dry off. You thank her, and the two of you embrace in the brilliant light of the sun and the blue sky. You are touched by the strength of the light shining from her heart, and you feel this reverberating throughout your entire body as a warm glow. She walks up the stairs in front of you, bowing as she leaves.

As the scene fades, you return to the center of the wheel, and we are now face-to-face.

THE RETURN

This is the center point. We are here where we began, fully aligned within the circle and within ourselves. The impact of the Twelve Initiations will continue to expand within you. Allow yourself time. Allow yourself contemplation. Allow yourself to simply BE.

When inspired, you may return to any initiation you choose. You may be drawn to a certain theme, or a certain number may reveal itself to you to experience again. Let the wisdom of the magic and the trust in what may appear to you as "random ideas" guide you to enjoy these as often as you like.

However, having gone through the Twelve Initiations now, you are initiated into a deeper level of self. This new knowing will begin to impact not only your thoughts and feelings, but also the physical body.

Allow the changes. Know that any discomfort is temporary. Seek care when needed, and nourish yourself with herbs and rest as you are guided from within, or by the healers and energy workers around you. Know that all is in flow, and change is also in flow, so what seems stuck or in pain now will move through its course, transmute, and disappear in perfect timing. Trust this if things should ever seem "off."

There is now a total recalibration occurring in all three of your energy bodies: the physical body, the heart/emotional body that surrounds you as a wider circle, and your greater mind-body that surrounds both of these—three concentric circles. As you move through life now, you may find rather quickly that you move quite a bit easier. However, remember to nourish yourself, to nurture yourself. Check in daily with your energy level. If it is low, know that the body and energy fields are assimilating this new vibration achieved through each initiation. And give yourself rest. If you feel you cannot, this is a great time to contemplate "why not?" This is a great moment to know that purely being is blessing this planet and all around you. This is a great moment to remember, "I need do nothing." What will really happen? What truth will be illuminated through this contemplation?

You Are. The powerful truth is that the gift of existence is the knowing of the experience of Being. Let the rush, the delight, the bliss of this knowing permeate your physical and energetic bodies whenever you can. You deserve this happiness! You deserve to live as pure joy. Your joyful vibration is the greatest gift you can offer to humanity, the planet, and the entire universe.

Bless you!

Bless your existence!

Bless you, great Creator God-Self!

You are Here!

You are!

You Are!

You ARE!

And so it is!

AHOM!

I love you.

ABOUT THE AUTHOR

A world-touring musician and lightworker who infuses life with creative energy, Luci Williams' journey began when she discovered Music Therapy at the University of Georgia. After graduation, she moved to New York City and teamed up with the Institute for Music and Neurologic Function, working with patients of all ages using music as medicine.

Luci was invited to play keyboards for Moby and traveled the world giving unforgettable concert experiences. She later joined the Trans-Siberian Orchestra for many years before choosing an independent creative life, awakening to her abilities to communicate with nonphysical energies during a trip to Bali in 2013. Through songwriting, meditation, and automatic writing, Luci became an open channel for a spectrum of teachers, guides, and masters of unconditional love.

It was during this time she met her husband, Sam Williams, who shared a similar vision of providing music to heal, activate, and empower audiences. Today, as an enlightened team, they lead transformational concerts, sound healing journeys, retreats, workshops, and classes focused on their dedication to creating more beauty and joy on Earth. To learn more about Luci, Sam, and their inspirational offerings, visit www.luciwilliams.com.

www.ingramcontent.com/pod-product-compliance
Lightning Source LLC
LaVergne TN
LVHW041943070526
838199LV00051BA/2889